I0456463

HERO
REDEFINED

HERO REDEFINED

PROFILES OF OLYMPIC
ATHLETES UNDER
THE RADAR

DOUG LEVY

CLEVER
CLEEVER

Copyright © 2025 by Doug Levy

All rights reserved.

No part of this book may be reproduced, or stored in a retrieval system, or transmitted in any form or by any means, electronic, mechanical, photocopying, recording, or otherwise, without express written permission of the publisher.

Published by Clever Cleever Publishing, Kenmore, Washington
AuthorDougLevy.com

Edited and designed by Girl Friday Productions
www.girlfridayproductions.com

Cover design: David Fassett
Project management: Sara Spees Addicott
Editorial production: Reshma Kooner
Image credits: cover © Shutterstock/Matheus Philip

ISBN (paperback): 979-8-9904983-0-3
ISBN (ebook): 979-8-9904983-1-0

Library of Congress Control Number: 2024918207

First edition

CONTENTS

INTRODUCTION

"It's the only time you can represent America and not have to carry a gun."

Former college basketball coaching great George Raveling said that to me back in 1984, when I interviewed him for a column on the Olympic Games that I wrote for the University of Oregon's school newspaper, the *Daily Emerald*. I love this quote because it captures the allure of the Olympic Games as an international stage where men and women come not to engage in war but simply to compete and to strive to do their very best for their country. They are there for noble reasons, putting themselves, their bodies, and their country's honor on the line.

I suspect that is why the Summer and Winter Olympic Games, which arrive every four years, have become a cathedral of sport, rising above the day-to-day athletics landscape. Australian swimmer and eight-time Olympic-medal-winner Dawn Fraser captured it this way: "The Olympics remain the most compelling search for excellence that exists in sport, and maybe in life itself."

Unfailingly, the advent of each Olympics, with the opening ceremony typically held inside the host country's Olympic Stadium, has a transfixing effect on all of us, bringing the kinds of chills and goose bumps that few other sporting events can. That sensation has come with thirty Summer and twenty-four Winter Olympics.

Yet for all the power, pageantry, and symbolism of the Olympics, I am struck by how little we remember about the Games, what we chronicle, and which names go in bold type to be retained in the annals of sporting history. The dozens of nations and thousands of athletes who compete every four years are reduced to a condensed version of where the Games were held, how a given site was chosen, and of course, who emerged as the most successful athletes, performers, and medal winners.

It is easy to read about the Games and find information on the various venues, costs, and top athletes, along with tables showing you how many gold, silver, and bronze medals each competing country took home. But, inevitably, most of the other details and stories behind the thousands of competitions and events have been compacted into a series of footnotes.

So, for the average viewer of all things Olympics, it is the winners—and even more so, the prolific winners—who strike the dominant poses in our mind's eye. Jesse Owens and Usain Bolt. Simone Biles and Nadia Comăneci. Sydney McLaughlin-Levrone and Noah Lyles. Katie Ledecky and Michael Phelps. Franz Klammer and Jean-Claude Killy. Mikaela Shiffrin and Lindsey Vonn. Sven Kramer and Apolo Ohno. Sonja Henie and Michelle Kwan.

In a way, it makes absolute sense for the public to remember these athletes as Olympic heroes. After all, they have walked that uncommon ground to a medal stand. They have persevered. And they have tasted victory, or something close to it—multiple times in some cases. They have racked up athletic achievements that so few others can claim. They are richly deserving of our attention and adulation.

But my goal in writing this book is to persuade readers to open their eyes a little more broadly, to enable a more expansive view of both the Olympic ideal and how we define heroism. Let's take a look at both those ideas.

First, the Olympics. They are absolutely about competition, but the International Olympic Committee (IOC) principles also speak to respect, friendship, and using sport, culture, and education to build a better world. That's why Antonio Colón, head of the Puerto Rico Winter Sports Federation, retains a beautiful memory of Russian and Ukrainian athletes sharing a conversation in the Olympic Village in 2022, mere weeks before Vladimir Putin ordered Russian troops to invade Ukraine.

On the competitive side, I love the succinct way four-time Olympic-discus-throwing-champion Al Oerter distilled what the Olympics meant to him. "I didn't set out to beat the world; I just set out to do my absolute best."

Pierre de Coubertin, one of those responsible for reviving the Olympic Games way back in the 1890s, captured that same essence of giving every ounce. "The most important thing in the Olympic Games is not winning but taking part; the essential thing in life is not conquering but fighting well." I don't think he was using *fighting* in a literal sense but rather to highlight the fact that, above winning, the Olympics is about giving your all.

Second, a key theme I explore in this book, and where I hope readers will adopt or at least be open to my broader view, involves the meaning of *heroism*. There are a variety of definitions of that word, with *bravery* and *courage* and *valor* most often sprinkled among them. But digging deeper, I learned that heroism is also defined as putting others first, or fighting on when others might give up. It can also mean protecting a principle and taking on challenges without any expectation of reward or personal gain. In other words, the essence of heroism goes beyond the men and women who enter a burning building or carry out a dangerous rescue mission. There is more to it than that.

To take it a step further, consider two monumental tragedies the United States and the world have endured: the September 11, 2001, assault on the World Trade Center towers in New York City and the March 2020 outbreak of the COVID-19 pandemic. Most Americans can readily visualize the heroes of the aftermath of 9/11. Think of the firefighters who entered burning towers, searched for weeks for bodies, and sacrificed their well-being for the greater good. With COVID-19, my mind drifts first to the doctors and nurses who strived to save as many patients as they could. Heroic, unquestionably. But what about the teachers who figured out a way, virtually overnight, to provide kids with education and care online? Or the delivery truck drivers who kept our grocery stores stocked? How about the restaurant operators who pivoted from table seating to takeout to keep their businesses afloat and their food safe to eat? Or the volunteers who helped at nursing homes and assisted-living facilities? Their sacrifices might be subtler, but I believe they, too, demonstrated heroism under fire.

In this book, I blend the Olympic Games and my expanded view of what constitutes heroism. There are thirteen chapters about Olympic athletes and other officials who demonstrated quiet heroism through resilience, strength of character, unparalleled sportsmanship, an incredible zeal to compete, and a seemingly superhuman and iron will to *finish*.

To me, the people in this book are heroes under the radar, because they typically came into our viewfinders for just a moment. They inspired stories and garnered media coverage, only to be later forgotten. A few were even the subject of books and, in two cases, film documentaries, but the books and films didn't receive major mainstream attention, leaving those athletes to also fade out of our psyches.

My hope is that you will see why the athletes in this book, as well as the creators and preservers of Olympic venues I profile, deserve so much more. The men and women on the following pages typically did *not* win any medals, and even the two who did demonstrated heroism that upstaged the medals they won.

A few of the Olympians featured here, like Manteo Mitchell, Gabriele Andersen-Schiess, David Moorcroft, and John Akhwari, showed unbelievable fortitude to finish races when many others might well have pushed the "Stop" button. Others, like Mel Wakabayashi and Peter Norman, faced racism and promoted human rights in their own ways. Still other athletes in this book exhibited an extraordinary ability to recover from horrific illnesses or injuries that threatened not only their athletic careers but also their lives. Read the stories of William and Charles Flaherty and Brian Stemmle to learn of the setbacks they overcame.

Just as athletes often need to navigate physical health challenges, there are times, too, when mental and psychological blows can stand in their way. Read about Tom Hintnaus and the psychological hit he took—and overcame.

I also explore the stories of two athletes, Tracy Barnes and Lawrence Lemieux, who exhibited heroism through selfless sportsmanship, even when it meant giving up their own dreams of Olympic medals.

Two chapters of this book are based not on Olympic athletes but rather on the heroism of people creating and restoring Olympic venues. One retells the story of the longshot bid to bring the Winter Olympic Games to a ski resort most hadn't heard of at the time—a bid that succeeded after being widely dismissed. The other involves the doggedness of a longtime luge coach in Sarajevo who was determined to rebuild a luge and bobsled track that had been decimated by war, pressing ahead even when volunteers and resources were in scarce supply.

Finally, there were a handful of athletes I had hopes of spotlighting but was unable to track down or interview for this book. Still, I wanted to note their acts of heroism. They are listed and briefly chronicled in a separate chapter toward the end of this book.

As you read about these athletes, the theme of sacrifice emerges in many of their chapters. I will readily confess their sacrifices don't involve putting their lives on the line or setting aside their own well-being for the benefit of others. But athletes routinely sacrifice enormous helpings of time for training, as well as their bodies, family lives, and social lives, all in the pursuit of excellence in their craft. So, too, do the people around them.

Now for another confession: This is not a scientific list. I sought out athletes from Summer and Winter Olympic Games who nearly always fell short of winning medals but who displayed the kind of fortitude, perseverance, sportsmanship, and respect for human rights that I found heroic.

That, of course, leaves some inspiring and deserving medal winners off these pages.

Just a few examples of medal winners I would label *heroic* in their actions include Dan Jansen, who speed skated to a gold medal in 1994 after failing to do so in three prior Winter Games and after enduring the death of his sister Jane to leukemia; Kerri Strug, who famously and gamely vaulted off an injured ankle in the 1996 Olympics, brilliantly preserving a team-gymnastics medal for the United States; and Joannie Rochette, a figure skater who bravely captured a surprise bronze medal in 2010 in her native country of Canada—two days after her mom died of a heart attack.

All three of these athletes displayed heroism and courage, and they are deserving of the accolades they received. I did not profile them only because their stories already burst into the mainstream, and they were appropriately and repeatedly spotlighted. So, too, were Olympians such as ski jumper Eddie "the Eagle" Edwards, the athletes from the first-ever bobsled team from Jamaica, and members of the 1980 US Hockey Team. They were all celebrated in the Hollywood-produced movies *Eddie the Eagle*, *Cool Runnings*, and *Miracle*.

The following pages, then, are reserved for athletes who may have left your memory bank or who perhaps never crept into your mind's eye in the first place. It is my hope that you will enjoy learning more about their stories, their achievements, and their quiet heroism.

I know I did.

PART I

DISPLAYING AN IRON WILL

CHAPTER 1

MANTEO MITCHELL, USA

4×400-METER RELAY, 2012
SUMMER OLYMPICS, LONDON

Dianna Ellis, Manteo Mitchell's mom, was used to seeing her oldest son running on a track, snapping his laser focus into place whenever he put his mind to the task at hand. "He's very headstrong," she said. "If he tells you he wants to do something, he's going to do it."

Manteo made a prophet of his mom on an August day in 2012, seconds after the starting gun went off for the 4×400-meter relay race in the 2012 Summer Olympic Games in London. He left a lasting impression in a way he couldn't have anticipated. But it would be only one of many occasions when Manteo impressed virtually everyone who came into his orbit.

Born July 6, 1987, in the town of Shelby, North Carolina, about forty-five miles west of Charlotte, Manteo remembered being constantly outside as a young kid. He grew up in a single-parent home, but he was surrounded by a larger family. "I grew up in an environment where, of our entire neighborhood, 95 percent of the people" were either older cousins or some type of extended family member. He played a lot among older kids and taught himself how to be mentally tough. "I learned how to swim by being thrown in the deep end."

Manteo was also quick to thank his physical-education teachers—Pam Fish and Bill Ellis, who has no relation to his mom—for encouraging him. Even a quarter of a century later, he easily recalled them and said he could recite the names of all his teachers. "He remembers everything and everybody from day one—it's amazing," said Dianna.

Like many kids, his first sports included basketball and football, and he was a very good athlete, quick and agile. But he had not yet discovered the sport that would become his calling card. When he was a junior in high school, Manteo began running only because his football receivers coach, Harvey McSwain, told his wideouts they needed to run track. McSwain knew a little something about the value of track and field, having helped anchor an NCAA-title-winning 4×100-meter relay team at North Carolina State University.

At the outset, Manteo wasn't exactly sold on the idea of running. "I knew it as a punishment for every other sport," he joked. Then, the summer before his senior year, he flourished. He sprinted the 400 meters in 50 seconds and the 200 meters in 22 seconds.

Manteo steered much of the credit for that toward McSwain. "If it wasn't for him, I wouldn't have run track and field." Whereas many of the high school football coaches these days are purely focused on that single sport, Manteo reaped the benefits of having a coach who had been a track-and-field athlete. And one who pushed his kids to run in good weather and bad. "If it was raining, we ran inside the school," Manteo remembered.

Still, scholarship offers weren't exactly raining down on Manteo as he prepared to transition from high school runner to college track and field. That was due not so much to his talent but to his status as a late bloomer. Additionally, he had always run on substandard tracks, many of them concrete.

Manteo vividly recalled a regional meet at Western Carolina University, about two hours away from him, as making a difference in his career. "It was the first time I had even run on an actual track, the first time where I felt good running and my legs didn't hurt." The results were dramatic. Manteo's sprints led his 4×100-meter and 4×200-meter relay teams to state records, and he also led his 4×400-meter team to victory. Oh, and just for good measure, he won the 400-meter and 200-meter races that day, too.

Manteo didn't know it right then, but another important coach—one who would become a major father figure in his life—was watching.

Danny Williamson, the longtime track-and-field coach at Western Carolina, remembered Travis Padgett as being the big draw at that meet. While Padgett would win the 100 meters that day, Williamson knew Western Carolina's chances of landing him were remote. "We were at best a mid-major [university]," he said. "We were not going to attract the number-one sprinter in the US. LSU, Clemson, Arkansas—that's the kid *they* get." Indeed, Padgett went on to star at Clemson University and advanced to the 2008 Olympic Trials, where he broke the NCAA collegiate record in the 100-meter qualifying heats with a time of 9.89 seconds.

But Williamson also took special notice of a kid who won a bevy of races. After the meet, he found Manteo and his mother and invited the young man to visit the Western Carolina campus the next week. Williamson said he left with a positive first impression of Manteo. "He was very well-mannered, like he really had things together," he said. "You could tell the love and respect he had for his mother."

The cloud of admiration from that meeting floated both ways, with Manteo appreciating the fact that Williamson took the time to come up to him. And the imprint Williamson has had on him has grown exponentially over the years. "He has had a huge impact on my life both on and off the track," Manteo said. "Most people call him Dubs, but I call him Pops, because he was my father figure. We talk all the time."

Manteo loved hearing that Williamson would let him pursue his love of music in school. He began his time at Western Carolina as a music major, and he still plays the organ, piano, and drums. His mom added that Manteo also sings well, but when pressed on that, Manteo said the melodious member of the family is his younger brother, Chazstein, a talented gospel musician. "I'll do the sports," Manteo said. "He can do the music."

From the beginning, the way Manteo ran for Western Carolina was music to Williamson's ears. "When he first started, his work ethic was that nothing was ever too much," Williamson said. "Anything I prescribed as his daily routine, he was like, 'I can do this.'"

To say Manteo was can-do for Williamson and Western Carolina's track program is a little like saying LeBron James threw down a few dunks. Manteo was all–Southern Conference and won his events, or wound up in the top three, more than thirty times. He was also the team's most valuable player four years in a row.

On the track, Manteo was ubiquitous, running both indoors and outdoors for the Western Carolina Catamounts. At two-day indoor meets, he ran the 60-meter, 200-meter, and 400-meter preliminaries on day one, and then the 60-, the 200-, the 400-, and the 4×400-meter relay races on day two. Outdoors, he ran the 400-, the 100-, the 200-, and the 4×100-meter and 4×400-meter relays on both days of a meet. He said if he had specialized, he "could have run so much faster." But by running in so many events, he knew he was helping his team. "I hated losing more than I loved winning," he said.

As Manteo finished up his Western Carolina track career in 2009, he began to focus more of his energy on the 400-, the 200-, and the 100-meter races. Manteo said he dropped a whole second off his 400-meter time (to 45 seconds) and 4/10th of a second off his 200-meter time (to 20 seconds flat). Then, in 2010, he ran a 10.04 in the 100 meters, which he said was later ratified as a 10.1. At that time, Manteo said, not a lot of track athletes specializing in longer sprints like the 400 were dipping below 10 seconds in the 100. As a result, Manteo's 100-meter time captured the attention of agents who signed him to a contract.

Soon, Manteo moved on to international competitions in Europe to test himself against some of the best sprinters in the world. That included a meet in Liège, Belgium, running the 400 meters and 4×400-meter relays against Belgium's Jonathan Borlée. A 400-meter entrant in the 2008, 2012, and 2016 Summer Games, Borlée won a 2009 NCAA championship for Florida State University and captured 4×400-meter-relay gold medals, running with his twin brother, Kevin, and later with his younger brother Dylan, in the 2012, 2016, and 2018 European championships. Manteo gained confidence when he finished third to Borlée and beat Kevin.

That confidence nosedived a year later, however, when Manteo went to the USA Track & Field Championships in 2011 at hallowed Hayward Field in Eugene, Oregon. "I got beat up," he said. "I worried

Manteo Mitchell looks fit and strong as he leads off the 4×400-meter relay for Team USA. But, an ominous challenge awaits. Credit: UPI/Alamy

about everything, including things I couldn't control." Digging into why that was, Manteo said that instead of focusing on his own race and what he needed to do, "I didn't control the race. I ran someone else's. I let the moment get too big mentally, and everything I'd done up to that point was thrown out the window in that race." Manteo also recalled that Jeremy Wariner, a three-time gold-medal winner, was in Lane 6, and he was in Lane 2. "I was just not ready," Manteo said, lamenting the fact that "Jeremy just took me on a boat ride." He didn't make it out of the 400-meter preliminaries.

Thinking back on what happened, he stressed "that *never* happened again my entire career." Although devastated, he consciously stayed through the end of the meet anyway. "I was just going to stay and tough it out. Stay and experience this—because I never wanted to see it again." At the end of the meet, he found an event brochure on the back stretch of Hayward and wrote a promise to himself on it: *The next time I come back here, I will experience the Hayward magic.*

Redemption came a year later in the 2012 Olympic Trials, which were, fittingly, at Hayward Field again. On the advice of Williamson, Manteo ran both the 400 and 200 meters. He set personal bests in both the 400 and 200 but knew, at that stage of his sprinting career, that the 400 offered him the best chance to make the Olympic team.

This time, Manteo was ready—maybe even *too* ready. He went out extremely fast, and at 330 meters, he still led LaShawn Merritt, the 2008 Games gold-medal winner. Merritt would ultimately overtake Manteo and win the Trials 400 meters. But Manteo had beaten Wariner, finished in fifth place, and—by milliseconds—qualified for the US 4×400-meter relay team going to London for the 2012 Games.

Before the pageantry of the actual Olympic Games, Manteo and other US track-and-field athletes went to a pre-Olympics meet in Canada. It went very well. His 4×400 relay team never lost, and he "came back with a shiny medal."

Next came London and a flurry of new experiences for the kid from a small town in North Carolina, who headed to the Olympics with a mix of emotions. "You have to go to a different world, a different mental space . . . You have the media, you have family, lots of egos." As they hung out at the Olympic Village, Manteo and his mom were in the same airspace as some of the biggest names in sports, seeing the likes of Kobe Bryant and Usain Bolt, the latter of whom would come to see Manteo under more trying circumstances just days later.

As the relays approached, injuries to US athletes made Manteo an even more vital member of the 4×400 relay team. Merritt pulled his hamstring in the 400-meter qualifying rounds and was taken off the relay team. Wariner pulled a quad muscle in a training session; he was out, too.

"After their injuries," Manteo said, "I just knew we had to step up in a big way. Those were the two defending Olympic champions from the last two Olympic Games. That's a big void in a sense. Our team outside of [Merritt and Wariner] was very young. I became the 'vet' of the squad." Yet Manteo emphasized he never felt fear or pressure, "just a sense of urgency to get the job done. I had to hold it down for my brothers and do my part for my teammates and for Team USA as a whole."

Looking to do his part, Manteo felt he was already in full-sprint mode—both on the track and off. Caught up in a beehive of activity, he had to take a shuttle bus everywhere, including to practices and team meetings, to spend time with family, and more.

Three days before the semifinal, in a seemingly innocuous way, Manteo had an injury scare of his own. It was August 6, and Manteo was returning to his apartment after a busy schedule of obligations. "I was running up [the stairs] to the second floor, and I tripped," he said. He had done something to his left leg and thought he might even have heard a snap. While he wasn't overly concerned, he did his due diligence. "I had it checked and got an x-ray," he said. "It didn't show anything."

When race day came, Manteo took to the track for the 4×400 semifinal. Along with his profound pride for being in an Olympic Games and representing his country, Manteo felt the pressure of getting his team off to a solid start: he had been selected to lead off the relay. "I was beyond ready," Manteo said. "I was super confident." He thought a time in the 43-to-44-second range might even be possible. Just to put Manteo's confident outlook in perspective, the world record in the 400 meters, set four years *later*, would be 43.03 seconds.

When the starting gun went off, Manteo was running well. Until he wasn't.

Manteo's great-aunt Pam was in the stands that day with Dianna, who had watched her son run for many years and knew what he was capable of. And she had a mother's intuition. "I told my aunt, Manteo's not running like he normally does." For many stressful minutes, she would have no idea why that was.

Nor would the manager for the 2012 USA Track & Field (USATF) team. Ken Brauman, a retired high school counselor who coached track athletes for over fifty years, was the USATF team manager. He paused from other duties to watch the 4×400 relay on the Olympic Stadium jumbotron. Seeing Manteo from a distance, he said, "You couldn't see that he was in any pain."

For Manteo, however, there was no ambiguity as to what was happening. At about the halfway mark of the 400, something went terribly, and audibly, wrong. "I felt and heard it," he said. The snap was audible to him, if not to others. He didn't know exactly what he had injured, but he knew the pain in his lower left leg was severe.

It would turn out that Manteo snapped his left fibula. Sometimes referred to as the calf bone, the fibula is the outer and smaller of the two bones between a person's knee and ankle. In layman's terms, Manteo had fractured part of his left leg, and he now had a mere nanosecond to make a decision of enormous consequence. He could stop. Or he could soldier on. Awaiting Manteo's relay baton handoff at the end of the 400-meter track was teammate Joshua Mance.

Mance had finished one place ahead of Manteo in the 2012 Olympic Trials in Eugene and knew only that his teammate had half a track still to cover. Tony McQuay would run the third 400 leg, and Bryshon Nellum, the third-place finisher in the Olympic Trials 400 meters, was prepared to anchor. On the jumbotron, Manteo noticed that Mance was motioning to him—one relay runner encouraging the other to bring the baton home.

In our interview, I pressed Manteo to look back and recreate this moment. I shared that I, and likely many others, would have screeched to a halt. Looking back, Manteo was fully aware that nobody would have thought a scintilla less of him had he stopped and stepped off the track. It would have been a natural, and easily explained, action to take.

But it would not be the path Manteo would take. A bundle of thoughts quickly came to him. The prevailing one was "what a huge honor" had been handed to him, and how he wouldn't, just *couldn't*, let his three teammates down.

"I have some of the fastest guys in the world depending on me," he recalled. "There are two choices: stop, or risk further injury." He reasoned that if he stopped, "no one would have thought anything of it. But there's one guy that would have thought something of it—and that's me."

The rest of us can only guess what it is like to run 200 meters at top-end speed on a broken fibula. Manteo lived it. He would be unable to turn in a world-class time, but he would not yield much ground, either. He was in Lane 3 and figured that he had to run somewhere between 45 and 45.9 seconds to keep a stacked team from the Bahamas within sight.

Incredibly, as it turned out, Manteo would run his opening leg of the 4×400 in 45.7 seconds. And his next two teammates picked him up. Race reports indicated that Mance's second leg pulled the USA team into contention and that McQuay's scintillating 43.4-second third leg gave them a temporary lead.

A Bahamian sprinter named Chris Brown would ultimately anchor his team to a semifinal win, though Manteo recalled it was later ruled a tie and the United States was declared the winner. In the finals, Ramon Miller anchored the Bahamas to a gold-medal finish, while the United States—with Angelo Taylor running in Manteo's place and anchoring—came in second.

So, after the semifinal race, had Manteo rationalized his opening 400 time with his teammates? Had he pointed to his leg? Had he shown them or told them what happened? After all, Manteo himself felt he would have run up to a second and a half faster on a healthy left leg. But there would be no "poor me" story.

In the moments after the race, he didn't tell his team what had happened. "I was very fortunate to have the headspace in the moment to fight through [the fractured fibula]." But Manteo had more than a casual walk in front of him. British officials had constructed a wooden stairway, a platform, and a tunnel from the track to the area known as the mixing zone, where athletes warmed up and cooled down, waited for one another, or received care from team doctors. Brauman recognized something was amiss only after Manteo grabbed his left leg and began a half crawl up the steps. Only when pressed directly did Manteo begin to drop some hints.

"He couldn't put any pressure [on his left leg]," Brauman said. "I asked him if he could walk, and he said, 'I'm sorry, I can't do that.'"

Manteo Mitchell prepares to hand the baton to teammate Joshua Mance as he finishes the opening leg of the 4×400 relay semifinals. Neither Mance, nor anyone else, knew at the time that Manteo had sprinted 200 meters with a fractured left fibula. Credit: Eric Feferberg / AFP / Getty Images

Brauman then escorted Manteo in a golf cart from the stadium to the mixing zone, where team officials gave him the medical attention he needed.

After a half century of coaching and managing elite track-and-field athletes, including eighteen different international teams and fifteen world championship squads, Brauman had no precedent to point to for this type of incident. "To be honest, I was amazed," he said. "I could think of plenty of world championships where people pulled a muscle and stopped and walked, but I had never witnessed anyone still *running* a race. I've never seen anything like it." As one comparison, there is British runner Derek Redmond, a former World and European Athletics Championships gold medalist in the 400 meters. Redmond earned justifiable applause for limping to the 400-meter finish line in the 1992 Summer Games in Barcelona after tearing a hamstring in the middle of the semifinals race. Still, he *walked* to the tape with his dad's assistance. Manteo had *run* to the finish line, alone.

Dr. Bob Adams served as team doctor for the USATF team during those 2012 Summer Games. Along with a pioneering doctor named Keith Peterson, he had established the first certified sports-medicine programs in the United States, helped start the initial drug-testing programs for track-and-field athletes in the United States, and spent twenty years as the man in charge of all USATF sports-medicine doctors. He said fibula fractures among elite track-and-field athletes are rare. Fractured tibias are more common, and with those types of injuries, it is extremely unlikely that a person can walk or put any weight on the bone.

In a morbid way then, was Manteo "lucky" to have fractured his fibula versus his tibia? Dr. Adams said in a sense it was, adding that his tripping incident on the stairway a few days before the race probably caused Manteo to sustain a fairly significant injury. But an athlete of Manteo's caliber instinctively knows how to taper down the use of the fibula to ensure that he doesn't run all out in the days leading up to a big race—in essence, to manage and minimize the pain. "He probably didn't challenge [the fibula]," Dr. Adams said. But clearly Manteo would have been in immense distress. "A broken bone is going to be painful." The job of the fibula is to support the ankle, and on a fractured fibula, "every rotation of the ankle is going to hurt." He added that the pain was exacerbated because Manteo was rotating that ankle around a curved and hard track. "It's hard to imagine the severity of the pain. It would be tremendous."

In retrospect, it was the mental acuity displayed by Manteo that impressed Dr. Adams just as much as his physical toughness. "He kept his composure under pressure, running for his teammates and his country. He had to be well-coached, he had to have self-discipline, he had to focus."

It would be midevening the next day before it all sunk in for the USATF athletes and officials, the news media and television cameras, and everyone else. NBC did a slow-motion isolation of Manteo's semi-final relay run and zeroed in on the part of the race when the fibula fracture occurred. When Manteo's teammates and other US athletes learned the full extent of what he had pushed through, there was a clear sense of awe. "I know among the athletes in the [Olympic] Village, it was, 'Can you believe he ran a race on a broken leg?'" Brauman said. "It was just amazing, just unbelievable."

For Dianna, the first thirty minutes post-race were agonizing. She didn't know what had happened to her son until she was eventually told he was being examined and x-rayed, and was then finally allowed to see Manteo. "It wasn't a good feeling, just standing there, seeing my son in pain, knowing there was nothing I could do." It was Manteo and his great-aunt who settled Dianna down. "He never complained about anything," Dianna said. "With some people, they'll go on and on—you know, 'This hurts' or 'That's killing me.' That's just not Manteo."

Dianna remembered the warm feeling afterward of having athletes as celebrated as Usain Bolt stop by to check in on her son. As more and more people stopped her in the airport after she picked Manteo up to bring him home, tension gave way to sheer admiration. "Everywhere you went, people spoke about it," she said. "People were just very excited."

One person who didn't spend a lot of time soaking in that excitement was Manteo himself. Dr. Adams remembered that Manteo made a seamless transition from model athlete to model teammate. For the 4×400 finals, Manteo limped down to the mixing zone to show up for his fellow relay runners. "When they came through, he was waiting for them. It's unusual, but he wanted to be there and support his friends.

Nobody saw that except for me. For him to go down there when he was hobbled, it says a lot."

Those 2012 Games would not be the end of Manteo's track-and-field career. He would, in fact, add the 300 meters to his repertoire, winning a gold medal in the event at the 2015 USATF Indoor Championships in Boston and a silver medal in the 300 at the 2019 USATF Indoor Championships in New York.

But track and field, especially the sprint races, is a young man's sport. Pretty soon, Manteo—the goal-setter, the laser-focused athlete—needed something else to satisfy his craving for challenges. There would be motivational speaking and coaching young kids, both of which he enjoyed, but neither lit Manteo's competitive fire. He needed something more.

The "something more"—the new challenge—came in the form of a contact from the chief executive officer of an Olympic sports program that Manteo knew nothing about. Manteo was headed to North Carolina's Outer Banks for his thirty-third birthday when a phone call came in from Aron McGuire, CEO of USA Bobsled/Skeleton. "I was like, 'Well, when we get back from the beach, I'll consider it,'" Manteo said.

It was no accident that McGuire had reached out to a track-and-field athlete—and specifically to Manteo. There were several shared experiences in their respective backgrounds that left McGuire confidently believing Manteo would respond enthusiastically to that phone call. En route to a secondary-education degree at the University of Akron, McGuire had been a hurdler who transitioned to the decathlon. He moved to Indianapolis after school to pursue his MBA from Indiana University, continued his decathlon training, and did a volunteer track-and-field coaching gig at Butler University. He would have loved to make an Olympic team in track and field, but he was realistic in knowing that would not happen.

McGuire knew a few decathletes who had made the crossover to bobsled, and he had seen the 1993 film *Cool Runnings*, based on the true story of a group of Jamaican sprinters who took up bobsledding and ultimately participated in the 1988, 1992, 1994, and 1998 Winter Games. He subsequently went to Lake Placid as one of thirty-three athletes who participated in a five- to six-day rookie camp, and afterward, he landed a spot on the USA Bobsled/Skeleton team, with whom he competed in national and world championship competitions. McGuire also worked at USATF from 2006 to 2013 and was at the 2012 Summer Games in London, where there was a buzz among the crew one evening after a certain 4×400 relay runner had sprinted 200 meters on a fractured left fibula.

Just as McGuire had suspected, Manteo would become smitten with bobsledding, especially after going to what he joked was "the middle of nowhere"—a frigid Lake Placid in the midst of the raging COVID-19 pandemic. "I literally fell in love with the sport," he said. "It was like NASCAR on ice." Beyond the racing, Manteo enjoyed the preparation and process of racing bobsleds. "Here I am again, putting in all the work—and all of that for 46 to 50 seconds."

McGuire said it's no accident that a track-and-field athlete, particularly one who specialized in short races, would have an affinity for bobsledding. There are only two major bobsled tracks in the United States—Lake Placid and Park City—so it is rare for USA Bobsled/Skeleton to see athletes who have spent their entire lives in that single sport. Much more typical, according to McGuire, is for the team to recruit athletes who are exceptional in track and field, football, volleyball, and softball, and who can transfer "fast-explosion" athleticism to bobsled.

Even so, McGuire said, those who gravitate to bobsled must pass a series of other tests that size up the athlete's physicality and ability to withstand the elements. He remembered an initial camp tested him in the squat, vertical jump, 20- and 40-meter sprints, weightlifting snatches, and more. Strength and speed are essential components to conquering the sport. "The start of a bobsled race is critical," he said. "It's like the first 40–50 yards of a track sprint."

But even if prospective bobsledders possess physical skills, McGuire said there is a second question they must answer. "Do they enjoy going down a track at ninety miles per hour in freezing-cold weather?" Only when an athlete gets to the track in the middle of an unforgiving winter can that second question be truly answered. McGuire said, "A lot of times it will be twenty or thirty [degrees] below [zero], and you're getting your body ready to compete at an elite level."

That weather component led Manteo's wife, Christina, to ask a key question: "Bobsled—are you serious?"

Dianna had a similar reaction. "Are you sure you want to do this? It's cold!"

But that was part of the lure for Manteo. "If there's something so far out there—'out of reach'—my ears perk up."

Still, Manteo acknowledged that the cold weather was jarring at first. "Coming from a summer sport, it was a very tough transition." Before going to his first combine, he bought a slew of gear on Amazon. "I took a jacket, heated gloves, socks, beanies. I ordered everything."

All that said, winter weather had found itself a fierce competitor, one used to overcoming the stiffest of challenges with his body and his mind. "A lot of people fall short of their goals not because they are not physically prepared but because they are not mentally prepared," Manteo said. And he placed a lofty goal alongside his mental preparation. He had, naturally, done some homework on his new winter sport, learning that only six athletes had won medals in both a Summer Olympic *and* a Winter Olympic Games. If Manteo was to make the US team for 2026 and earn a medal, he would be the seventh person—and the first African American male ever.

There would be much work ahead before he could get to that point, such as trips to the 2024 and 2025 World Cups in Lake Placid. And then he would need to be selected for the USA Bobsled/Skeleton team heading to the 2026 Winter Games in Milano Cortina, Italy.

Manteo said he has performed well in his new sport, with a couple of podium finishes at competitions and plenty of times where he finished in the top six in the four-man bobsled. And McGuire has kept a close eye on the athlete he helped recruit. "He's a push athlete, and one of his strengths is his top-end speed," McGuire said. "It really benefits the team." He also praised Manteo's mental makeup. "Manteo has a tremendous mindset. There are things he can take from his level of success. He's been able to pull teams together, pull athletes together."

But while McGuire acknowledged that Manteo Mitchell is "on a short list of athletes to be on the Olympic team," he emphasized there would be no guarantees. Manteo's commitment would have to be all in.

Somehow, I doubt Manteo would ever expect anything to be

handed to him. I also got the real sense that Manteo would be content with who he is and whatever he does, medals or no medals. In fact, he ranked his 200 meters of running on a fractured fibula above the accomplishment of winning a relay-team silver medal.

"It's at the top," he said. The Olympics is the mountaintop for track athletes, and Manteo said it is a great feeling "to know you inspired a generation." Another gift from his experience was that he went from being a shy kid to an adult at ease with public and motivational speaking before audiences at businesses, schools, churches, and more. "I was given this pedestal," he said. "It's a story that is generational, and it can be used in so many situations."

That story will always stick with Dr. Adams as well. People often ask him who his favorite track-and-field athlete was, and while it is a thankless question to answer, Manteo ranks way up there. "It was one of the most memorable track-and-field events I ever saw. What he did in that setting was amazing. I've worked with a lot of tough athletes. They play with pain, but in the athletic field, his performance stands out. It was exceptional."

I came away from my interviews with Manteo, his mom, and his inner circle convinced that his accomplishments have stretched beyond his athletic ability. He seems to have performed the roles of citizen, community leader, husband, and dad as seamlessly as he ran on a track or pushed a bobsled. He has a son, Khi, and he and his wife welcomed a new baby girl, Melody Joy, into the world in 2023.

It was telling that Manteo's longtime coach, Williamson, talked about him less as a track or bobsled athlete and more as a complete human being. "This is a very bright and intelligent young man who cares about everyone. He would do anything for anyone. He works with kids all the time, he is a great father, and he is a great guy," Williamson said. "If you were an adult and had a son, I'm pretty sure you'd want your son to be like Manteo."

CHAPTER 2

GABRIELE ANDERSEN-SCHIESS, SWITZERLAND

WOMEN'S MARATHON, 1984 SUMMER OLYMPICS, LOS ANGELES

Erich Steinbock and his wife, Judy, have been vacationing with their good friends Gabriele "Gabi" Andersen-Schiess and her husband, Dick Andersen, for decades now. The get-togethers include yearly trips to the warm desert air of Palm Springs, California, where, on arrival, the Steinbocks invariably spot a stockpile of exercise equipment for Gabi.

Steinbock said that equipment speaks loudly to Gabriele's tenacity and commitment to staying fit and pushing through. He said while he, his wife, and Dick are all devoted to exercise, Gabriele takes it to an entirely different level. "One thing about Gabi—she pushes through everything. There always seems to be one extra mile, one extra ski run. When other people are done working out, she will go to the fitness center. She *just doesn't stop.*"

If you were to rewind to August 5, 1984, and compose an anthem to express the ordeal Gabriele Andersen-Schiess endured on that scorching Los Angeles day, you couldn't pick more immaculate lyrics than the words uttered by Steinbock.

Before we get to Gabriele's heroic moment in time, let's first review the backstory of this Swiss distance runner. She was born on March 20, 1945, in Thun, Switzerland, a picturesque village in the shadow of the Bernese Alps, where organized school sports and competitive opportunities for women were limited in those post–World War II days. During her youth, she enjoyed skiing, hiking, and judo, and it wasn't until she was in her midtwenties that serious running came into her life. By then, she had graduated from the University of Zurich with a degree in history and art history. As Gabriele progressed toward an advanced degree in physical education, she began running with friends, some of whom were members of a track club. Gabriele was intrigued.

"The longest distance [to run] was 1,500 meters," she recalled about the time period. "There were a lot of races they didn't let women run." Gabriele wasn't a sprinter, so she stuck to the 1,500-meter races, eventually progressing to the 3,000 meters when that event came to the scene in the 1970s.

Gabriele is unassuming about this segment of her distance-running career—about everything, really. "She doesn't like talking about herself," Dick said. He pointed out that the place where she attained her advanced physical education degree in 1973, Eidgenössische Technische Hochschule Zürich (ETH Zurich), has quite a pedigree. It's the institution where a sixteen-year-old named Albert Einstein, who would go on to develop the theory of relativity, first distinguished himself in physics and mathematics.

While seeking her advanced degree, Gabriele began to work with Jean-François Pahud. In 1972, Pahud had dual roles at the Swiss Championships in Geneva, running the 1,000 meters as an athlete and helping coach Gabriele, along with other top long-distance runners from the French-speaking regions of Switzerland. Gabriele won Switzerland's national title in the 3,000 meters that year.

Then, she further burnished her reputation with Pahud the next year when she finished as the runner-up at Switzerland's Cross Country Championships in both the 1,500 and 3,000 meters. The only runner who bested her? The great Marijke Moser, who had run the 1,500 for Switzerland in the 1972 Summer Olympics in Munich, Germany.

While Gabriele had clearly established herself as a runner by 1973, she received a tip that year that would help her find her true calling: long distance. "A coach said there's this marathon," she recalled. "I went, and I enjoyed it—and I did pretty well." Racing in a pair of sweats along the dirt roads that made up the Black Forest Marathon course, Gabriele covered the 26.2 miles (42.195 kilometers) in a little over 3 hours.

While that time may not sound elite to today's sports enthusiasts, it's important to remember that the first woman to officially run the Boston Marathon in 1967 finished it with a time of 4:20:00 (4 hours, 20 minutes, 0 seconds). Bear in mind, too, that Gabriele ran on a standard roadway, well before the design of aerodynamic running wear that helped men and women lower their times. Gabriele's early success in the marathon convinced the lifelong skier to throw more of her energy into this newly adopted sport. She upped the ante even further in late 1974 by moving to the United States, where the distance-running boom was entering full bloom.

At that point in her career, Gabriele lacked the type of structured training and instruction that elite women distance runners take for granted nowadays. "I didn't really have a coach," she said, referring to her early days in the United States. But in lieu of a coach, she found a different lifelong partner to help her marathon running reach new heights.

It began with Gabriele's longing to see the Grand Canyon. As it turned out, there was a ski area a little over an hour's drive from the natural wonderland, so one day she decided to hitchhike up. The man who gave her a ride offered her a job by the time they got to the top of the mountain, and that's where Gabriele, as the new ski instructor, met Dick, a student at nearby Northern Arizona University in Flagstaff.

The initial meeting had a bit of a rocky beginning. "I was working my way through school," Dick said. He had also become a ski instructor, which earned him a free pass to the Arizona Snowbowl. One day, he had all his kids practicing on a bunny hill when they found themselves behind a group coached by Gabriele. Her students cut in front of his.

"She put her kids right in front of me," he said. "I thought, *Who's this woman who doesn't know how to position her students?*"

Gabriele Andersen-Schiess was thrilled to be part of the Swiss team and reveled in attending the 1984 Summer Games' opening ceremonies. Credit: Dick Andersen

Dick and Gabriele would resolve their differences soon enough, though, to the point where he began giving her regular rides to Flagstaff, and she began taking his dog for runs. The rest, as they say, is history. The two wed in March 1975, and they have been married ever since.

With her husband rooting her on and encouraging her to take marathoning more seriously, Gabriele, a self-coached runner, progressed on an upward arc. Of course, in true Gabriele form—and using her own words—she also "dabbled" in swimming and cross-country skiing. Her résumé showed that she excelled in these sports, too: she was a member of a Nordic ski team, won a Great American Ski Chase Series in 1980, and finished runner-up in an NBC Sports "Survival of the Fittest" event in 1982.

It turned out that 1982 would be a banner year for Gabriele. One of her goals was to run the Pikes Peak Marathon, which she entered and won in August. The next year, she and Dick were working at Sun Valley Resort in Idaho and met a man who was headed to Boise for a major marathon. Gabriele went, too, and her performance on that course served as a watershed point. She finished in just under 2:44:00.

"That's when the light went on," Dick said, "that she might be pretty good at this stuff."

If that marathon gave Gabriele a taste of how good she could be, then the information she gleaned from her native Switzerland served as an even more attractive appetizer. While Gabriele had achieved US citizenship in 1978, she was also eligible to run for her home country, and that nation's Olympic standard required her to run under 2:37:00—well within her reach.

The timing of Gabriele's meteoric rise in marathoning was sublime in yet another way: the 1984 Summer Games in Los Angeles was just around the corner and would feature the first women's marathon. This was a significant step forward for the Games, especially considering it came only a dozen years after the Amateur Athletic Union had removed a ban on women entering distance races and allowed women to register for marathons.

In the lead-up to the 1984 Summer Games, Gabriele followed her virtuoso 1982 success with an equally impressive 1983 string of marathon finishes. She came in second in an event in San Francisco, then won the October 1983 Twin Cities Marathon with a qualifying time of 2:36:18. She topped that with an even better performance at the California International Marathon in Sacramento two months later, clocking what was then a Swiss national record of 2:33:25.

At this point, Gabriele was turning enough heads to receive a shoe deal from Adidas and to be thought of as a marathoner that coaches wanted to develop further. She wound up working out with a coach in the distance-running mecca of Eugene, Oregon: Bill Dellinger.

Dellinger, who competed in the 5,000 meters in three Olympic Games and won a bronze medal at one of them, had succeeded the legendary Bill Bowerman as head track-and-field coach at the University of Oregon in 1972. During his twenty-five-year tenure as the head man for the Oregon Ducks, he would go on to lead his team to five NCAA titles and help his athletes attain 108 All-America honors.

Aside from Dellinger, Gabriele also received coaching from long-distance running savant Bob Sevene, who would spend many years as the head coach of Nike's Athletics West track-and-field club, working with more than seventy-five professional athletes. Of those, twenty-three competed in the 1984 Summer Games, including Gabriele and world-record holder Joan Benoit.

As the Summer Games drew closer, Gabriele was not considered a favorite. But she had demonstrated herself as a marathoner to be reckoned with, and in April 1984, she proved to Switzerland's officials that she could run a high-quality time in a major race by snagging a sixth-place finish in the prestigious Boston Marathon with a time of 2:39:00.

Gabriele said, "I knew I wouldn't be fast enough to medal, but I hoped to finish in the first half [of the women marathoners in the 1984 Games]."

By then, Gabriele was thirty-nine years old and over the moon about competing in the Summer Games. "I was ecstatic," she said. "I had never thought about actually being in the Olympics—especially at my age." Other than a British female athlete who ran the women's marathon at age forty-six, Gabriele was one of the oldest Olympians among those gathered in Los Angeles.

As if preparing for the Summer Games didn't bring on enough stress for her, Dick inadvertently added to it one day when he left his wallet on top of the chauffeur's car on their way into the Olympic Village. After that, he and Gabriele went their separate ways, with Dick and his close friend Steinbock soaking up their spare time in the land of Hollywood and Walt Disney. They discovered what most people who travel to Los Angeles in August or who permanently live there instinctively know—how thick, hot, and muggy it can be.

What few understand, however, is how tough a chore running over 42 kilometers in those conditions can be. And the weather conditions weren't the only problem; the city's smoggy skies made breathing a laborious effort for all the athletes—and especially for the distance runners.

So, as excited as Dick, Steinbock, and especially Gabriele may have been, and as much as they viewed this inaugural women's marathon as a celebration for women athletes, the conditions in LA were about to deliver some challenging blows. In retrospect, Gabriele said she might not have appreciated those challenges fully enough. Pahud was again coaching her and thought she'd trained very well. He was reassured

When Gabriele Andersen-Schiess entered the Olympic Stadium, lurching from side to side, it was clear something was very wrong. Credit: Colorsport/Shutterstock

of her fitness level during a 20-kilometer run on July 27, less than two weeks before the marathon. Yet he was concerned when Gabriele ditched a run the next day in favor of standing in the sun for several hours for the opening ceremonies of the Games. He fretted, too, that she then flew back to Sun Valley to train in cooler weather during the last several pre-race days instead of better acclimating herself to the warmer and muggier conditions in Los Angeles.

At the time, however, those worries seemed trivial. On the morning of the race, and after it was underway, Pahud indicated that Gabriele appeared stress-free.

Those were positive signals—and Gabriele one-upped those signals with an even better one at the 30-kilometer (18.64-mile) mark. Having posted himself there to gauge Gabriele's progress and fitness, Pahud saw a Swiss marathoner striding confidently. She hadn't forgotten to hydrate. And she was only 7 minutes and 45 seconds behind the leader, Benoit. All seemed to be going smoothly, so Pahud stepped away from the racecourse and moved to the Los Angeles Memorial Coliseum, where he watched the end of the marathon. He parked himself with several colleagues in a section of the stadium reserved for the athletes.

Meanwhile, Dick and Steinbock had worked out their game plan as well. They were pumped up during the warmups and had rented mopeds so they could easily track Gabriele and her progress during the first half of the race. They remained amped up, Dick said, when Gabriele found herself among the top fifteen runners a little past the halfway point. With plenty of pep in her step, the two men also headed to the Coliseum and their seats to watch the end.

But cracks were forming in Gabriele's armor. For one thing, the day that began as overcast quickly turned sticky and hot. Though it was still early morning and marathoners had been on the course for only an hour, the temperature had already risen to eighty-three degrees Fahrenheit. Then, the heat struck with a vengeance, the temperature ultimately ramping up to ninety degrees by the close of the race, accompanied by an uncharacteristically high 95 percent humidity.

Besides trekking through the heat, Gabriele and her fellow competitors carried other burdens as they ran in the inaugural women's Olympic marathon. The course, Dick said, was one that put runners under direct sunlight and at some points traversed a freeway, which radiated heat off its pavement. In addition to that challenge was a more fundamental one: a lack of water.

Nowadays, water stations are an omnipresent part and parcel of courses hosting marathons, half-marathons, and long-distance events around the world. But for that hot and smoggy first women's Olympic marathon in August 1984, race officials were not as prepared with hydration stations. To be clear, there were a handful of them, but they certainly were not posted every mile. "Back then, there were only five [stations]," Gabriele recalled.

That, combined with the overall conditions, created significant challenges for even the most accomplished runners. Six of them failed to complete the marathon, including world-class distance runners like New Zealand's Anne Audain, a Commonwealth Games 3,000-meter winner just two years prior.

In Gabriele's case, a race that had gone so according to plan for about 24 miles would, she acknowledged, "fall apart." She didn't remember *why* she missed the final water station, but she did, and as a result, severe dehydration would soon set in.

At the time, however, no one could have known the toll the temperature, the smog, and the distance would take on her heat-ravaged body.

Steinbock was still coming off the high from the news that, as he recalled, Gabriele had risen as high as eighth place at mile 20. But as he and Dick waited anxiously for her to come into view, they felt a sense of foreboding. With the rising temperatures and the packed stands, the LA Memorial Coliseum stadium "was much warmer than it was out on the course," Dick said. He started to see other runners coming into the stadium whom Gabriele had run ahead of earlier in the race. "People are coming in and coming in, and I'm getting worried," he recounted. There was no sign of Gabriele.

"We were sitting there, and she doesn't come in," Steinbock added. "Doesn't come in. Doesn't come in." They both knew something was off-kilter.

As runners continued to arrive, the spectators in the stadium were carrying on a marathon tradition that had begun well over a century ago in 1896, when competitors began their course in a town called Marathon and completed their last laps in Athens's Panathenaic Stadium. There, the roar of the crowd helped propel them through that last lap and change. This day was no exception.

Benoit had entered the stadium first to a deafening noise. The Maine native proved that her world-record run in the prior year's Boston Marathon was a harbinger of greater things to come, as she finished with a sterling time of 2:24:52. The 1983 World Champion, Grete Waitz of Norway, followed for silver. Rosa Mota of Portugal finished third.

On this day, though, what transpired about twenty minutes later would in some ways render the medal winners as footnotes. A historical finish of a different sort was about to play out.

Pahud wrote that "abruptly everything changed" when Gabriele entered the Olympic Stadium. Steinbock remembered, "At first, there was a roar, and then it became very quiet."

Gabriele was on the stadium track, but she wasn't running. She was

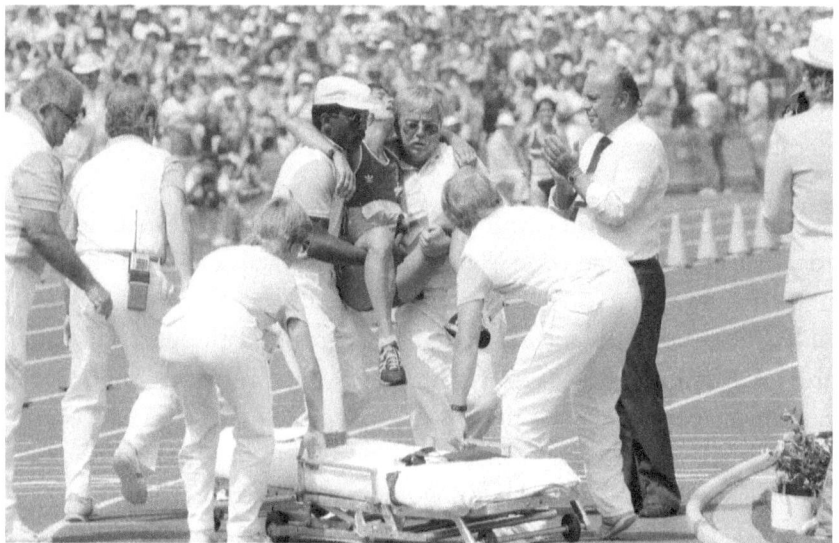

Gabriela Andersen-Schiess is lowered onto a gurney at the Los Angeles Memorial Coliseum after she finished the women's marathon and collapsed. Credit: Dieter Endlicher / AP Images

lurching from side to side, taking one painful step after another. Her head was tilted and her steps distorted, with an awkward gait extending her legs across multiple lanes. Her complete exhaustion was palpable.

Doctors on the side of the track immediately wanted to help, but Gabriele waved them off, because accepting medical aid would disqualify her. This rule dated back to 1908, when an Italian runner named Dorando Pietri staggered and fell to the track near the close of the London Games marathon, with a doctor and a race official rushing to his aid. Pietri was disqualified and lost a gold medal.

As Gabriele waved off her would-be helpers, she had spectators, race officials, and everyone else on high alarm. One spectator sitting in the stands in front of Steinbock and Dick made a fuss over how terrible Gabriele looked. Dick started thinking he should get down on the track to try to stop her. "But she would have been very upset."

On the track, Gabriele *just wouldn't stop.* As she showcased a display of grit, willpower, fortitude, and steely determination, the Los Angeles crowd rose to its feet and began to roar for an agonizing 5 minutes and 44 seconds, which Pahud described as the "5:44 that assaulted me."

That final lap took Gabriele over 4 minutes longer than most elite runners take. She was experiencing the kind of pain that, for most humans, would have triggered every fiber to yell and scream at them to stop. That cry would have been heeded by 99.99 percent of us. But something inside Gabriele kept her going. She wasn't like everyone else. Gabriele was the 0.01 percent.

Steinbock wryly called her stagger to the finish "the Gabriele Andersen finishing kick," but the rest of those who witnessed her extraordinary bout of perseverance praised her with more reverential reviews. After Gabriele recovered, she found a series of media trailers set up with droves of reporters wanting to talk to her. "A guy told us that was the most reporters he had seen," Dick said.

One column writer later dubbed Gabriele's lap of fame "The Most Incredible Final Lap in Olympic Marathon History." George Vecsey of the *New York Times* wrote a post-race column headlined "First Gasps, Then Cheers," in which he likened her to a powerful, but nearly defeated, beast.

> Some people would compare her to a boxer out on his feet, but she looked more like a brave bull after the picadors have done their cruel business. In the brutal "sport" of boxing, no athlete would be allowed to continue twisted out of shape as she was, but the opponent in distance running is not external but internal— the sheer will to finish. It is the beauty of this event but also the danger.

Was Gabriele in significant medical danger? Doctors beside the track determined otherwise, seeing that Gabriele was still perspiring and thus had not suffered heat stroke. They would not intervene—yet. But they did rush to her aid immediately after she took her final step across the finish line. They covered her in ice and towels and gave her intravenous fluids. Incredibly, within two to three hours, she said she felt fine, but Pahud recalled an excruciating wait of over six hours before they could "claim her and bring her back to the Swiss delegation."

Looking back four decades, Gabriele wished it had been legal to get water or to be hosed down. And although she appreciated that her performance may have generated empowerment for other women athletes, she did not see anything particularly heroic in what she achieved. That outlook was an example of the self-deprecation that lives side-by-side with the competitive fire breathing inside her. In fact, she actually confessed to some embarrassment. "I couldn't quite understand the hoopla," she said. Of the images and videos of her final lap that inevitably arise whenever her name comes up, she said it's not that pleasant. "You know, you wish you'd look a little better."

The beauty of her achievement was, of course, not in the looks but in the sheer struggle. She finished in 2:48:44, a time still good enough to place thirty-seventh out of forty-four runners. For context, that time, even accounting for Gabriele's limping final lap, was faster than those the men's gold-medal winner had run in the first five Olympic marathons. Moreover, Gabriele had inspired more women to run, to compete, to *finish*.

Still, to Gabriele, it has long remained a head-scratcher that so many people recall the feat even while forgetting other details of the event, including who actually won the marathon. Yet for her family, her friends, and society, those Summer Games represented remarkable resilience that has transcended time and continued to touch deep chords of emotion. And her performance embodied an impressive level of fortitude and an unbelievable willpower to overcome severe odds, simply to finish. Yes, what she did was heroic in nature.

Both Steinbock and Dick have marveled at just how unbelievably Gabriele has performed over the years since those Summer Games across an array of physical activities, and they've talked about how much better she could have been with early training, coaching, and guidance. "She would've been a tremendous triathlete," Steinbock said. In her youth, Gabriele had excelled in running, biking, skiing, and swimming, and after knee surgery forced an end to her distance-running career in 1991, she started whitewater kayaking, snowboarding, and mountain biking. She also participated in several skiing marathons, won multiple medals in cross-country skiing, and captured first place in a mountain-biking championship in July 1999.

She continued to compete well into her late seventies. And even then, the world, both nationally and internationally, has retained a strong interest in her.

In Osaka, she has been invited to be the grand marshal of yearly parades and has been featured in a television show remembering the 1984 Summer Games alongside three other famous Olympians—Carl Lewis, Edwin Moses, and Mary Lou Retton. She was also featured with Moses at the Olympic Museum's thirtieth-anniversary tribute to the 1984 Olympics, held in Lausanne, Switzerland. A French author named Marie-Claire Gross published a book in 2018 titled *5 Minutes 44* in which she detailed in romantic fashion the tortured final minutes of Gabriele's 1984 marathon run. And every four years, as the Summer Olympics beckons, she "starts to get calls," according to Dick. For the 1988 buildup, officials flew her to Seoul; prior to Tokyo, a crew from Japan came to film her.

Gabriele's impact has also been profound on those with whom she worked closely, including Pahud. Over the years, he became a renowned coach who spent eight years in charge of Switzerland's middle- and long-distance runners. He also coached a Bahraini running star named Maryam Jamal, who won five Asian Games championships, two world championships, and a 2012 Summer Olympic Games gold medal in the 1,500 meters.

While Pahud coached some of the best, the email relationship he has maintained with Gabriele—and the reunion meeting they had in May 2023—held a special place of pride and joy for him. "Sport is not only the performance, the joy of victory, or the pain of defeat," he wrote. I think what he meant is that some performances go beyond recorded wins or losses; they inspire us to *feel* something. With Gabriele's 1984 marathon, that was clearly the case. She finished near the back of the pack that day, and yet at the same time, she evoked in so many people a powerful and long-lasting awe from seeing someone so determined to finish and to overcome obstacles in her path.

Steinbock also emphasized Gabriele's influence on him. "Gabriele has been an inspiration for me, my wife, and many of our friends," he said, explaining that her pattern of cloaking her achievements in characteristic modesty and humility is a hallmark of growing up and living in her homeland. Steinbock described a 2008 book about the search for happiness: *The Geography of Bliss* by Eric Weiner. "The Swiss do not like to create envy," Steinbock said. "They are not selfish or egocentric people." Getting Gabriele to talk about her accomplishments in running, biking, and skiing, he said, is a virtual no-go "unless you bring it up. And then it is like you asked about the weather."

Steinbock was about to say more. First, though, he paused midway through our phone interview to tell his wife he was talking to a writer about Gabriele. Judy's two-word reply provided an apt finishing touch to a story that began with her husband's well-chosen words about their close friend.

"She's unbelievable."

CHAPTER 3

DAVID MOORCROFT, GREAT BRITAIN

5,000 METERS, 1984 SUMMER OLYMPICS, LOS ANGELES

Even forty years later, the 1984 Olympics in Los Angeles was a traumatic subject for David Moorcroft. "It took me a long time to be able to talk about LA," he said.

When David did harken back to those Summer Games and his performance in the 5,000-meter final, the words tumbling out of his mouth were the stuff of Greek tragedy. He spoke of "deep disappointment" from which he "never recovered." He acknowledged he was "totally embarrassed." He referred to the finish line of that race as being "quite a lonely place."

It is odd, then—if not downright unthinkable—to square David's 1984 finish with the one he experienced twenty-five months earlier. For in July 1982, the snapshot of David on a track in Oslo, Norway, reflected a scene of exquisite triumph.

Taking stock of his performance that day, I found no distance runners outside Africa who ran a world-best time in the 5k since David did so. It is not a stretch to characterize this English athlete as among the world's best middle- and long-distance runners ever, and certainly one of the most elite from an era that was a veritable who's who of middle- and long-distance runners.

How, then, to reconcile these competing portraits of David? We can learn more by talking to the man and those around him. We can view the picture in more depth by delving into the physical ailments that never seemed to fully subside. We can review the successful aftermath of all the pain, all the extraordinary highs that jogged beside the lowest of lows. And we can wonder if David's deep disappointment was instead worthy of respect and applause in its own right.

David Moorcroft was born on April 10, 1953, in Coventry, a city at the center of the United Kingdom some two hours away from London. As a kid, he wasn't athletically gifted or a physical specimen, but he could run well. Of course, part of the learning process of being a runner is understanding that someone, somewhere, is bound to run faster than you on any given day.

In an autobiography he cowrote after his 1982 run in the 5,000 meters titled *Dave Moorcroft: Running Commentary*, David described how he'd once felt after finishing last in a school cross-country race. He had compounded the agony by hurting his foot. "I was shattered. Desolate. Inconsolable. And twelve."

Although a running-club official set David straight with some prescient advice that runners have to "learn very quickly how to lose," it didn't happen to David very often, especially after he connected with a legendary running coach at age sixteen. It was then, in May 1969, that David came under John Anderson's tutelage. Anderson helped David scale heights that were unimaginable to him up to that point.

Ironically, Anderson was best known to many Brits as the head official appearing on the well-known television game show *Gladiators* from 1992 to 2000. But track and field was his true North Star, and earlier in his career, he had served as a national coach for the Amateur Athletic Association of England and as Scotland's first full-time national coach. From 1964 to 2000, Anderson would go on to coach a track-and-field Olympian at every Olympic Games and would tutor five world-record holders.

"I regard him as a genius in so many ways," David said. "I absolutely know I wouldn't have been the athlete or person I am without him. At his best, he is a brilliant mind—articulate, analytical, incisive, inspirational, and many other adjectives."

Anderson thought highly of David as well. "It was obvious to me from literally the start that David was no ordinary schoolboy. I knew that he was going to be special." Their coach-and-pupil relationship quickly transitioned into a partnership, and Anderson believed that it was up to David to envision what distance he wanted to do. He also appreciated how David often barraged him with questions, wanting to know *why* he was doing what Anderson trained him to do. "Every athlete you come across should be a replica of him."

But while Anderson lit the fire that would fuel David's running career, it was a flame of a different sort who would become his partner in life.

Linda Ward first met David at Tile Hill College of Further Education in Coventry. He was seventeen years old, and she was sixteen. She was at the college to take a secretarial class, while he was retaking what was called an "O-Level" class. They started dating in earnest in 1971, and, Linda said, "It was six months before I realized he was a pretty good runner."

It soon became clear to her that her boyfriend was much more than just the "enthusiastic jogger" she labeled herself. "He trained twice a day," she said. "I just became used to it, and we molded our days around it."

The molding experiment stuck. Linda and David wed in 1975, had two children, and have been together ever since. Her husband's running has continued ever since, too, though Linda applauded David for figuring out how to balance his home life and competitive life. "He was so dedicated to training, but we always tried to fit it into family things. It's just part of everything we'd always known—part of our everyday routine."

It became routine, too, for David to excel on the track. He wrote in his autobiography that he ran the equivalent of a 4:04 mile as an eighteen-year-old, leading to an invitation to run in a prestigious 1971 event called the Emsley Carr Mile. There, he met Brendan Foster, one of a cadre of distance runners who spearheaded a 1970s and 1980s renaissance in track and field for Great Britain and who represented his country in the 1972 Summer Olympics in Munich.

Just weeks after setting a world record in the 5,000 meters, David Moorcroft nearly notched another, defeating a stacked field in a 3,000-meter run at Crystal Palace. Credit: Phil Sheldon / Popperfoto via Getty Images

David ran well over the next year and beyond, including a personal best of 3:45.07 in the 1,500 meters, but he did not make the British team for the 1972 Summer Games. Still, his running career was kicking into high gear, and in 1975, it ramped up even more.

David ran a 3:42.02 in the 1,500 and broke the 4-minute-mile barrier for the first time, finishing fourth in a meet where the top three finishers were middle-distance-running royalty: John Walker of New Zealand, Mike Boit of Kenya, and Marty Liquori of the United States. He then trained maniacally for the next year, entering a stacked 1,500-meter field in Britain's Olympic Trials to determine that country's Olympic Games lineup. He finished second with a personal record of 3:39.09 to make the team—and wrote in his autobiography that one of the also-rans back then was a guy named Sebastian Coe. History assured us Coe would not be an also-ran for long. "I knew then there was something special," David said.

At the 1976 Summer Olympics in Montreal, David finished a very respectable seventh, clocking a time of 3:40.94. Two years later, he won a Commonwealth Games gold medal in the 1,500 with a swift 3:35.48. But his days of focusing on the 1,500 meters were winding down.

Through consultation with Anderson and some soul-searching over the next few years, and with recognition of the caliber of Great Britain's 1,500-meter runners—world-class athletes like Coe and Steve Ovett—David ultimately decided to transition to the 5,000 meters. His 1979 race against Coe, when his competitor and friend sped to a world record, cemented his decision to gravitate to the longer distance.

During the years leading up to the 1980 Summer Games in Moscow, David combined his ongoing training with a few years of broadening his horizons, professionally and socially. He and his wife went to New Zealand, where both accepted jobs as teachers and where David met two men who became lifelong friends. One would become a business partner as well.

Tony Rogers, an up-and-coming middle-distance runner for New Zealand, raced against David in a 1,000-meter event and ended up becoming a daily training partner. Together, they took relaxing morning runs along the lush, green riverbanks of Hamilton and in a picturesque town called Huntley. Meanwhile, David also taught social studies at

Saint Paul's Collegiate School in Hamilton, where a thirteen-year-old named Paul Breed was one of his students.

"He was a much better bloody athlete than he was a teacher," cracked Breed. "I'm not sure he knew what the bloody hell social studies *was*." But Breed soon found out that David was one helluva runner. One day, Breed was in a meet with eleven other intermediate, junior, and senior schoolboy runners who ran alternating legs around the track, while David used all twelve legs as a training run. At one point, David casually cruised up beside Breed, who said he'd been "running flat-out." But the student made an impression, and at a subsequent parent-teacher conference, David mentioned to the boy's folks that, as a runner, Breed had "some real style about him. If he wants some guidance, have him come see me."

Suffice it to say the boy did. "Forty-six years later, we're the best of friends," Breed said. He came to think of David as a lifelong role model, too. "Everybody has people in their lives who are guiding mentors. I learned so many values from him."

In 1980, the last full year he and Linda lived in New Zealand, David won a Moscow Olympic Games qualifying event in the 1,500. He subsequently decided not to run that event and later qualified in the 5,000—barely. However, he was struggling with severe calf pains and a stomach virus, and he didn't make the 5,000-meter final. As he wrote in his autobiography, he didn't even stay in Moscow to watch. "The Olympic history books will record I took part, and not much else."

David was hardly the first distance runner to confront an injury at the Olympic Games or to fail to make a final; distance running can be grueling, and dozens of runners enter Olympic Games distance events only to miss qualifying for the finals. David has acknowledged that many runners as talented as he was never fulfilled their potential due to injury, noting how greats like Coe and Steve Cram fought their share of injuries as well.

Still, he berated himself for what he viewed as his failure in Moscow. "I was my biggest critic and always struggled to be satisfied," he said. "I was more competitive than I realized, and I was just not good at not winning."

But while the 1980 Summer Games performance would lead David to beat himself up mentally, what is just as telling is that the Moscow Olympics marked one of several time frames when his body absorbed a more significant beating than his mind did.

"I was quite an injured athlete," he said, labeling himself "very fragile." In fairness, David was slight of build, packing hundreds of miles of training into every month, and competing nationally and internationally against some of the best middle- and long-distance runners in track-and-field history. "I was always on that tightrope of trying to achieve great fitness without being injured."

All that took its toll.

The litany of physical challenges David fought through would make a medical team's jaws drop. Stress fractures in his foot. Operations on both calves. Hernias. A series of painful groin, pelvis, and pubic-bone injuries. Lower-back pain that impacted two of his vertebrae. Liver problems. Sinus infections. And more. In his autobiography, David included a shirtless picture of himself with a diagram of all the injuries, surgeries, and beaten-up body parts that undermined his race-day fitness throughout his career.

Most of those injuries, excluding the ones to his groin, pelvis, and pubic bones, had occurred in one form or another before he participated in the Bislett Games in Oslo on Wednesday, July 7, 1982. But leading up to that evening, David had enjoyed a several-months-long streak of injury-free and productive training. "The best winter I ever had," he said. He described himself as "masochistic and aggressive" in his workouts and "training like a lunatic." Linda said she knew David "was in the [best] shape of his life." Having run a mile under 3:50.00, he was peaking to the point that Anderson predicted his prized runner was ready to do something special and run 5,000 meters in the low-13-minute range.

Did he ever.

The air was electric that night in Oslo. In one of the races leading up to the 5,000 meters, American Steve Scott ran the mile in 3:47.69—only 36/100ths of a second off Coe's world record. Then came the 5,000, where David would crank up the voltage even further. He lined up against a talented field that included Henry Rono, who had set a world record in the event only the year before.

Harboring hopes of threatening the 13:14.06 British record, David took off like a shot and never really let up. In a stunning video clip of the race, viewers can see that there was absolutely no one challenging David over the last several minutes of the race. He strode confidently and smoothly, almost smiling, as he brandished his country's blue jersey.

"It was one of those occasions where you can't put a foot wrong," he said, "when you're flowing and flying along and light as a feather." He had learned to expect pain and fatigue, and to fight through it toward the end of a distance race, but the pain scarcely arrived that night. All those physical beatdowns off the track and the frustrating setbacks on it leading up to this race helped make David's performance even more remarkable. "One of those perfect runs."

As David approached the bell lap of the race, the clock in the stadium showed only 12 minutes, and he turned in a 58.04-second final lap to cap it off. He had not only obliterated the world record, but he had also nearly dipped below the 13-minute mark, finishing with a time of 13:00.41. What left track-and-field experts and fellow runners even more flabbergasted was that David had destroyed a world-record holder without any "rabbit" in the race, meaning a pacesetter who takes off quickly to assure faster times and typically drops out well before the finish. Rono was never a factor in this 5,000.

"I'd never seen anything like it," said Eamonn Martin, a longtime friend and fellow Olympian with a Commonwealth Games gold medal and London Marathon win on his résumé. Martin said David "ran away and ran easy" and "produced an absolutely monumental performance." Had a rabbit gone out quickly, he added, David "clearly would have broken 13 minutes."

It did not take long for the late-night world-record-setting performance to reverberate around the European continent. Linda, who had decided not to accompany her husband to Oslo, received a call from Foster, who had been in London with a British Broadcasting Corporation (BBC) television crew that was overseeing event coverage. "Guess what your husband has just done?" he asked her. "Set a British record?" "No," he said. "More."

Asked how he reacted to the news as David's coach, Anderson said, "You mean after I came down from the ceiling?"

Those post-world-record days were crazy ones for the household,

Linda said. Among other things, her husband was "inundated with phone calls," and a horde of reporters from the British media huddled outside the front door when she and David would return home. Somehow, David and Linda, then in their late twenties, had the kind of maturity to take it all in stride. "We were both old enough that we could put it into perspective," she said.

Only ten short days after setting that 5,000-meter world record in Oslo, David went to the famed Crystal Palace in South London to compete in a star-studded 3,000-meter race. The world-class runners lined up with him included Ovett, Scott, Walker, Sydney Maree of South Africa, and Boit and Peter Koech of Kenya. This time there *was* a rabbit at the start, and at the end, David and Maree staged a duel for the ages.

Maree tried to pass David with 300 meters to go, and the Brit held him off, but with 200 meters left, the South African surged ahead. Conventional wisdom would tell you that Maree put on his ferocious finishing kick, and that was that. But conventional wisdom would not have accounted for a home crowd roaring for their newly minted world-record holder to summon up one last burst.

The video of the race is spellbinding. Both David and Maree were in white singlets, separating themselves from the rest of the field as the final lap beckoned. The capacity crowd at Crystal Palace, some 24,000 fans, seemed to add decibels and octaves to the din with each tactical move by the runners.

Maree looked to pass David right near the start of the bell lap, and David held him off. Roar number one. Then Maree *did* pass, but race announcers correctly predicted he had gone too fast too soon. David kicked confidently past Maree—roar number two. And then David lengthened his lead by several yards as he reached the finish line—a final roar.

The crowd reveled in David's victory lap, and he had plenty of time to enjoy it, since the 3,000 was the last race of the evening. "It was the most enjoyable victory lap I've ever taken and the best connection with a crowd that I ever made," David said. He won the race with a time of 7:32.79—just over three-quarters of a second off Rono's four-year-old world record of 7:32.01.

Martin and Breed both believed that David's Crystal Palace 3,000 might have been more impressive than his world record, given the competition it came against. David agreed. "[It's] the race I'm most proud of," he said, flatly.

David continued to make waves, turning in more impressive times over the next two weeks as he entered 800-meter and 1,500-meter events to get in some speed training. He ran personal bests in both— 1:46.64 in the 800 and 3:33.79 in the 1,500. In those four weeks, he had recorded lifetime bests in five events, a world record in his specialty, and a near world record in the 3,000.

It could be extraordinarily tempting to wonder what we would have witnessed had 1982 been an Olympic year. After all, David was at the height of his career, as physically fit, as injury-free, and as celebrated as he had ever been. One news account dubbed him the "Fourth Beatle" of British middle- and long-distance runners of his era, along with Coe, Ovett, and a young Cram—who would later set three world records during a nineteen-day span in 1985. It was the high-water mark of an idyllic decade where British middle- and long-distance runners regularly set, broke, and held world records at every distance event between 800 and 5,000 meters.

"If the Olympics had been in July 1982," David said, "that would have been great." But for track-and-field athletes, it is a cruel fate that, just as often as not, the Olympic Games come along at less-than-ideal points in time. "You rarely go into it in the best possible condition."

There would never be a reigniting of the blazes that flared in the summer of 1982, when David lit the track-and-field circuit on fire. He would win another Commonwealth Games gold medal, this time in the 5,000, in October 1982. But 1983 and 1984 would be injury-plagued years, with more operations, cortisone shots, and a new barrage of groin, pelvic, and pubic-bone injuries attacking his body in the spring of 1984. "I managed to get through May, June, and July with a minimum amount of racing," David said, adding that he won a 1-mile tune-up event in Oslo that gave him some renewed hope.

Then it came time for the 5,000-meter race at the 1984 Summer Games in Los Angeles. The competitors had to deal with soaring temperatures during the heats on Wednesday, the semifinals on Thursday, and the final on Saturday. "I was really struggling, and it was extremely painful—like a hernia," David said. "It did cross my mind not to race as I was warming up. I felt a lot of doubt."

But David said he chased the doubt out of his mind. "I knew that it was likely to be my last Olympic Games, and so the only option I had to try and be an Olympic champion was to run the race."

Martin ran in that same 5,000-meter final and contended with the same conditions as David but had the benefit of being over five years younger. He was convinced that the three-races-in-four-days gauntlet disproportionately impacted his injured friend. "I think two races would have suited him much better," Martin said. Linda added that David "really didn't want three races. He thought he could hold it together for two."

Perhaps the final blow to David's chances was the pace of the 1984 5,000-meter final. Sometimes, 5,000- and 10,000-meter races at an Olympic Games can turn methodical and tactical, meaning runners back off their pace to seize a strategic advantage over their opponents. Others move at a more breakneck pace from start to finish. This Olympic final was the latter. "It was a really fast race," recalled Martin, who started in the lead pack but struggled at 3,000 meters and ultimately faded to thirteenth place out of fourteen runners.

In the stands of the Olympic Stadium, a pregnant Linda had gathered with David's parents, Anderson, and their two-year-old son, Paul, who enthusiastically called for his dad. "We told [others in the stands] who [David] was," Linda said. "So people all around us were excited about the race."

But as the 5,000 progressed, it became clear that this would not be David's day. Far from it.

"As Dave went further and further back, it got quiet," Linda said. "People were really embarrassed. I was sad for them, and they were sad for us. It was devastating. We'd all worked toward it, and then . . ." This 5,000-meter final came six days after the women's marathon event where Gabriele Andersen-Schiess had experienced the devastating effects of severe dehydration and lurched to a finish. Unlike her experience, there wasn't a noticeable come-apart moment for David. But there would also be no giddyup, no rally, no pick-me-up part of the race. Just immense distress. David had felt the pre-race pain and experienced the pre-race doubts that led him to at least question if he should go through with this race. But while Linda understood her husband was battling multiple injuries, David didn't confide to any of the other runners the kind of searing stabs of pain he felt in his pelvis, a pain so intense that he could have—and perhaps in the minds of some, *should* have—stepped off the track before those 5,000 meters were up.

It did not occur to him then, but David was putting on a heroic display of fortitude and guts even as he limped to the end in fourteenth place—last among those who had entered the race. His struggle did not go unnoticed, especially by the renowned producer of Olympic Games documentaries Bud Greenspan. Greenspan instructed his cameramen to keep the lens trained on the runner who, only two years earlier, had smashed a world record in the 5,000 and was now forcing himself through hellacious pain and desperately trying to avoid being lapped.

Greenspan quoted David as having said, post-race, "Look, maybe it will change. You die before you pull out of the Olympics." Although David later allowed that the quote was probably accurate, he believed Greenspan had "made it quite dramatic. It wasn't quite so." To the viewer, it didn't *look* dramatic in the way that Gabriele Andersen-Schiess's marathon finish had because David didn't break down or grimace. He acknowledged, though, that mentally he "was shattered."

But to friends like Breed, a special quality of David's—a quiet brand of determination—had shown itself. "There was no way that Dave wasn't going to finish the race, come what may. He would have had to have been dragged off the track before he would have stepped off," Breed said.

Indeed, David spent an entire career finishing every race he ran, this one included, and looking back, it was a record he was proud of. The goal of finishing, no matter what, had been ingrained in him from his earliest days of running. He described the objectives of a race as such: you try to win, you do the best you can, and you finish. "I always thought, I have to finish, because as soon as you didn't finish, you give yourself the option that you don't have to, going forward." So, at the time, David would not concede that he had done anything remotely special. He had finished with a time of 14:16.61—more than 76 seconds off the world-record pace of the 1982 race in Oslo, and what he wanted most was to get off the track, to become invisible.

A look at David Moorcroft's post-race expression reveals a portrait of a runner who fought through injuries, pain, and disappointment. Credit: Colorsport/Shutterstock

Linda had navigated all the highs and lows of David's running career. Now she had to wrestle again with how to communicate with a husband who was consistently tougher on himself than anyone else could ever be. "That's always been the most difficult thing, and the best thing to say, really, is nothing. I was incredibly disappointed and devastated for him. We knew it was our dream, our last chance," she said, indicating that both she and David knew there might well not be another Olympic Games for him. But this was not a time for Linda to display or speak of disappointment. "I couldn't show him any of that. I had to be normal, to carry on as I always do. Saying too much would have been so much worse."

David described the 1984 final of the 5,000 in LA and the two to three weeks immediately after as "like a death in the family." What helped David most was to retreat to that family. He joined his wife and son for a next-day outing to Knott's Berry Farm, an amusement park south of LA, where they managed to laugh at a puzzled two-year-old son who asked, innocently, "Why didn't those men run with you, daddy?"

David benefited, too, from the fact that the British media did not jump down his throat. None of the people I interviewed remembered any harsh coverage at all. That's probably because, for one thing, David commanded respect not only as a top-flight competitor and a world-class runner but also as a true gentleman and a nice guy of the sport. For another thing, the 1984 Games would see Great Britain pile up its most prolific stack of medals since the 1920 Summer Games. There would be thirty-seven in all, including gold for Coe in the 1,500, for Daley Thompson in the decathlon, and for Tessa Sanderson in the women's javelin.

David said that over the next two to three years, he eventually found perspective and appreciation. The guy who was used to being so hard on himself learned the value of reflection and self-esteem. "The world moves on, life moves on," he said. "I'm very proud of not drop-ping out, and really glad I didn't." David also realized that, in terms of 1984, he had just competed in his third consecutive Summer Games, where the facilities are chock-full of athletes who *didn't* medal. "By definition, you walk around the [Olympic] Village, and there are a few people who are ecstatic, but many more who are miserable as sin."

Besides, there was a long list of people who saw David's experience from the same camera angle that Greenspan did. Breed and Rogers were two of them. "How many other people, suffering that intensity of agony, *wouldn't* have stepped off that track?" asked Breed. "Think of the mindset of the guy. He doesn't come off the track and start blurt-ing about being hurt. He doesn't need to put out headlines about nurs-ing an injury. It's not in his psyche to talk about it beforehand or use it as an excuse afterward. It's just not the way he's built."

Rogers pointed out that David was sick much of the time they trained together in 1983, dealing with a virus and giardia and back problems. In 1984, as they took training runs through the Olympic Village, around a veterans' cemetery, and on Wilshire Boulevard, David mentioned to Rogers that he was experiencing some physical problems and getting treatment. "He was struggling a bit, that's for sure," Rogers said, but he emphasized that his friend "was hugely mod-est about what he endured. It was only after he had surgery in 1985 that you realize what he went through."

What David endured would have positive side effects, too. "Sometimes, we both believe in fate," Linda said, adding that if the 1984 Games had been a smashing medal success for her husband, "our lives may have gone in a completely different direction. We may not have been as happy . . . and we may not have been able to see his potential."

Instead, David and Linda see his 1984 Olympics experience as one that hastened an important metamorphosis for a thirty-one-year-old runner—a career evolution that has enabled him to achieve as much success away from the track as he'd sustained on it.

Even before the 1984 Summer Olympics came along, David had been doing broadcasting work for BBC, and he expanded that work through the 1980s and much of the 1990s. He subsequently provided track-and-field commentary for the Canadian Broadcasting Corporation (CBC) as well.

In 1997, David became head of what had been the British Athletic Federation and is now UK Athletics, the governing body of track and field for the United Kingdom. When David came onto the scene, UK Athletics was downtrodden and on the brink of bankruptcy. During his decade as the organization's chief executive, the fortunes turned. When he eventually left the organization, Linda said, her husband had just secured a sponsorship of nearly £50 million over six years from British insurance giant Aviva. That's the modern-day equivalent of more than £90 million, or just under $114 million.

But above and beyond his broadcasting work and the resuscitation of UK Athletics, the crown jewel of David's adult life—and certainly the endeavor closest to his heart—is his work in developing the Coventry Sports Foundation. After fifteen years serving as chief executive of that charitable organization, he stayed on as chair of the board of trustees of CV Life, a charitable organization whose mission is to advance community sports and culture, and that represents the partnership of the Coventry Sports Foundation and the Culture Coventry Trust.

Just as importantly, he helped recruit the man he taught, coached, and befriended all those years ago in New Zealand. In part through David's persuasion, Breed moved to the United Kingdom in 1988 and never left. Then, in the mid-1990s, Breed took over the reins as chief executive officer of Coventry Sports Foundation, ultimately becoming CEO of Culture Coventry and CV Life as well.

"He said, 'I'd love for you and I to work together,'" recalled Breed, who marveled at David's passion for helping those struggling with life's challenges. "The guy has a real deep-seated passion for addressing inequalities and underrepresentation in communities where people don't enjoy the breadth of opportunities that both he and I have."

Breed said that he and David shaped the entirety of Culture Coventry Trust out of nothing, and CV Life developed an enormous reach and breadth of activities. Its community development efforts have included work on sheltered housing, food programs, and much more. One particularly significant project arose in connection with the London Summer Olympics in 2012. The organization developed a program called Africa Inspires to help raise funding for the construction and opening of a 30,000-liter water-harvesting tank to provide fresh and clean drinking water for kids in five schools in Kampala, Uganda.

Charitable and professional endeavors aside, David's track shoes are never fully put away. He remained an avid runner long after his competitive days were over, and as a track-and-field coach, he helped Breed earn a place on New Zealand's team for the 1990 Commonwealth Games in Auckland. Although Breed raced in the 800-meter heats of those 1990 Games, he didn't make the final, and that outcome became a source of some back-and-forth smack talk between lifelong friends. "I absolutely rip him to shreds about LA, and he does the same with me with Auckland," Breed joked.

Beneath the light-hearted jabs, though, it was abundantly clear that Breed, athletes like Martin and Rogers, and David's coach, Anderson, all retained a special reverence for David the runner and David the man. Those Olympic Game journeys didn't turn out the way David had wanted them to, but the people who knew him best said that it shouldn't detract from his overall legacy.

"Dave had some terrific achievements," said Rogers, who became head of the Athletics Wellington track-and-field organization in his home country of New Zealand and who cohosted a regular podcast about the sport called *Chew the F.A.T* (referring to "Field and Track"). He said the life David breathed back into UK Athletics "should be as much a legacy as his feats on the track," adding that "everybody is always appreciative of spending time with him, and that's the true measure of the man and his family."

Martin said of David: "He broke the world record, and he would have been under 13 (minutes) had anybody challenged him. The guy's talent from the 1,500 through the 5,000 was phenomenal." He said those who look at Olympic results and downplay David's accomplishments need a reintroduction to the magnificence of 1982. "We have to remember what he did in between [the years of the Olympic Games]. He was a shining light. When other big names were not having good years, *he* was the phenomenon."

Anderson said, "I don't want to give the impression that David is holier than thou," but he added that "David is very much a man who people would want to admire and copy from. I don't think you can do anything more outstanding than be an example for others to emulate."

That kind of lofty praise is much more likely to come from others than from David himself. He joked that two knee replacements and advancing age turned him into a distance-running slowpoke. He and Linda beamed as they talked about a recent 5k run where three generations of Moorcrofts—David and Linda, their kids, and their grandkids—ran together. Linda thought *she* had run last, but David insisted it was he who had brought up the rear. "I did an LA," he cracked.

Along with the self-deprecating humor, David also achieved a certain peace of mind. He will never entirely divorce the disappointments from his memories, yet as horrible as the 1984 experience in LA was, he said, "It taught me to love running again. It's just a privilege to be able to do it." When asked about his career on balance, he said, "If I put down on paper all the things that have gone well and those that didn't, the list of those that went well would be a lot longer. I absolutely don't think I'm the victim. My life's been pretty good."

CHAPTER 4

JOHN STEPHEN AKHWARI, TANZANIA

MEN'S MARATHON, 1968 SUMMER OLYMPICS, MEXICO CITY

"Mr. Levy!"

The booming voice belonged to the gentleman dismounting the back of the motorcycle. John Stephen Akhwari, dressed in a bright-green Tanzania team tracksuit, looked fit and trim, as if he could run another marathon. Over a half century ago, he had run one for the ages.

John represented Tanzania in the 42-kilometer (26.2-mile) men's marathon at the 1968 Summer Olympics in Mexico City. He didn't bring a medal back to his native country. He did, however, use every fiber of energy he had, demonstrating an incredible level of intestinal fortitude and gutsiness. It gnaws at him that a dwindling number of people remember.

"He went to visit the National Museum [of Tanzania] about five years ago, and he couldn't find any information about what he had done," said Ayoub Laizer, the interpreter for my interview with John. Officials who accompanied John "introduced him to the guys at the

Running with a bandaged right knee from a dislocation and severe cramps, John Stephen Akhwari still manages to finish the 1968 Olympic men's marathon. Credit: adsR/Alamy

museum, and the museum workers knew nothing. Very few people know about him—so it's a bit sad."

I sat down with John to learn more about his exploits leading up to and on October 20, 1968. That's the day the men's marathon was staged at the 1968 Summer Games, which were held from the twelfth to the twenty-seventh of October to match up with the time of year when temperatures are more comfortable in Mexico's capital city.

My wife, Teri, and I met John in person in his home country after nineteen hours of flying from Seattle, Washington, to the Kilimanjaro International Airport outside of Arusha, Tanzania. Our meeting spot was Gibb's Farm, a converted coffee plantation situated near Lake Manyara National Park and the Ngorongoro Crater. Gibb's Farm was one of three safari camps we stayed at during a nine-day trip to Tanzania, which offered the kind of close encounters with and eye-popping views of the natural wildlife it is so well-known for.

The fact that we caught up to John and were able to sit across from him constituted a minor miracle. I had tried traditional routes to obtain contact information for him, but outreach to the Tanzania Olympic Committee and Athletics Tanzania, the country's governing body for track and field, did not yield any leads.

Somehow, staff from the touring company we used for our trip, Go2Africa, managed to track down email information for the youngest of John's eight children, Josephine Stephen, who lived in Dar es Salaam, the largest city in Tanzania, located on the east coast, some 779 kilometers, or a little under 500 miles, from Gibb's Farm. Through Josephine's graciousness, patience, and organizational skills, as well as a helping hand from Kim Sher of Go2Africa, a meetup was arranged within seventy miles of John's home in what is called the Mbulu District. John used automobile and motorcycle drivers to get to our interview. Then, after our interview, dinner, and an overnight stay at Gibb's Farm, he reversed the process to get home.

"Mr. Akhwari, it is an honor to meet you!" I said.

"It is an honor to meet you!" he replied.

In preparation for our interview, John had packed a duffel bag of documents and certificates to frame a career of running, military service, and farming that involved both heartwarming triumphs and soul-crushing setbacks. He had medals, too, with a quote inscribed on one of them that perfectly captured the essence of the struggle he'd waged in the thin air of Mexico City more than a half century earlier.

John was born March 27, 1938, in the same Mbulu District where he still lives. His parents farmed, and he also settled into farming, as well as into a marriage that lasted well over fifty years. But before that came a love of running, one that began when John was a schoolboy, spurred by the incentive of a free soda.

Organizers of a 15-kilometer race at John's school used free soda to get students to participate. It became the first of many for John, and, sure enough, he earned a bottle of Coca-Cola after he finished fortieth out of seventy runners. The young jogger caught a tantalizing glimpse of what distance running could do for him.

"Getting that Coca-Cola, for him, was something he wouldn't forget. It was an opportunity that kept him running," Laizer said.

The bounty got more impressive in 1960 when John finished first in a field of ninety participants running a 10-kilometer race in his town. That time, the prizes were a blanket, a bottle of Cinzano, and twenty British pounds. He also won a regional 3-mile race that year, both 3-mile and 6-mile races at a 1961 tournament, and a 1-mile race in 1962.

Later in 1962, John got his first taste of marathoning—and it was clear he had an appetite for it. He won an East African tournament run in Kenya's capital city of Nairobi and took home the first of many trophies he would amass over the years. These victories motivated him. *I should keep doing this*, he thought.

The impressive run in Nairobi attracted the kind of notice that would enable John to compete on an international scale. More top-shelf finishes followed: sixth-place at the 1962 Commonwealth Games in Perth; second place in a Sri Lanka event in 1963; and runner-up at an international marathon in Greece, which happened to be sponsored by the same soft-drink corporation, Coca-Cola, that had helped him acquire the running bug in the first place.

For that run in Greece, John received a certificate, a trophy, a $1,000 check—and a rude awakening to how officials in a just-forming country felt about a commoner winning $1,000. Although Tanzania sits on one of the oldest continuously inhabited spaces on Earth, the country itself was relatively young after declaring its independence from the British monarchy in 1961 and then merging with the newly formed Zanzibar in April 1964. Having just broken free from an aristocracy, the country wanted to be seen as the champion of the working class. It therefore might not have cast such a kind eye on a twenty-something marathoner being awarded a then-princely sum of $1,000.

"After he won second place, he came back to Dar es Salaam and met the minister of sport," Laizer said. "When he was posing for a photo, the minister grabbed the check and put it in his pocket." John had planned to purchase a couple of buses and start a transportation business, and that money could have changed his life. But, as Lazier explains, "He had no way to complain . . . He didn't know anyone to help him go get his money back." John's dream of a free enterprise was taken away from him.

John could have been thrown badly off course by what happened to his cash prize from Greece, but he didn't skip a beat on the competitive trail. In 1968, he won an African Nations Championship in Uganda, and he was also part of an Outward Bound group that climbed Mount Kilimanjaro. Those endeavors provided some preparation for a Summer Olympics run in high-altitude Mexico City, but not enough. John said his country's track-and-field leadership made a head-scratching decision by sending him and other Tanzanian marathoners to train in Dar es Salaam, only 121 feet above sea level. The marathon in Mexico City would involve running on a 26.2-mile course at an altitude of more than 7,000 feet.

The decision not to train Tanzania's Olympic distance runners at altitude invites a number of questions. Why not have the Tanzanian marathoners train in the vicinity of Mount Kilimanjaro, which towers 19,341 feet above sea level—or at least *somewhere* in the mountainous and densely forested northeast portion of the country? Or why not give marathoners advance time to adapt to the altitude, temperature, and humidity of Mexico City? These are some of the look-back questions for which we likely will never have solid answers.

Despite all that, John headed to Mexico City in 1968 as a battle-tested marathoner. He was used to winning marathons, or at least finishing in the top ten. But such good fortune would not smile down on John in October 1968.

The marathon began at the famed Zócalo, the central square that has for five hundred years served as a vibrant heartbeat of Mexico City. One of four athletes in the Tanzanian delegation, John was assigned running bib number thirty-six.

Somewhere between the start of the race and the close of it, John sustained a severe injury to his right leg. But the answers to exactly *where* that occurred and *how* it happened are not open and shut.

John said in our interview that his injury occurred 30 kilometers into a 42-kilometer marathon. He got a severe muscle cramp, dislocated his knee at that point, and temporarily fell to the pavement in pain. As he recalled, first-aid officials helped him tape up his leg, and he continued on. But this triggers a question that is difficult to decipher the answer to. International Olympic rules have historically precluded competitors from getting external assistance or medical aid during an event. Had race officials simply supplied tape that John then used to bandage his injured right leg? Had he brought his own tape with him? The year 1968 was a long time ago, and records on an issue like this are nearly impossible to track down. I located a longtime rules official for USATF who verified the rule but was unsure exactly what may have happened.

John did say that someone beckoned him to get in a car, which would have been a clear disqualification. "No . . . I'm here to finish the marathon," he'd responded.

As for the question of precisely when and how the injury happened, a Wikipedia write-up indicated it occurred at the halfway point of the marathon, that it involved jostling, and that John fell and dislocated a joint in his knee. This explanation would have meant that John ran some *13 miles* with a severe injury, versus the *7.5-mile* distance he had described. But the Wikipedia account didn't cite any verifiable sources, and I couldn't track down any despite reaching out to five different track-and-field and sports-writing organizations.

What seems most likely, then, is the account of John's injury that he has consistently shared with his family and friends, namely that the cramping at 30 kilometers led to his fall, his pain, and his dislocated knee. And regardless of whether this happened with more than half a marathon to go or with only 12 kilometers (7.5 miles) in front of him, John was running in an event that dishes out particularly harsh treatment to the human body. The toll of the injury on his body, combined with the heat and humidity that all the runners had to confront, had to have been immense.

In some ways, only those who have experienced the marathoner's journey firsthand—as I had in 1983 and again in 2014—can truly understand just how mightily the 26.2-mile event taxes runners physically and mentally. But in a 2018 article, the respected running magazine *Runner's World* helped define what the race is like by chronicling a

Even at age 85, John Stephen Akhwari looks fit and trim in his Team Tanzania warmup jacket. Credit: Doug Levy

litany of potential physical ailments in store for those who take that 26.2-mile-long journey: runny nose, cramps, nausea, blackened and/ or lost toenails, sore feet, lost water weight, and even a temporary loss of height.

As for the severe leg cramp John suffered, a publication called *Runner's Blueprint* described the effects of it this way: "When cramps strike, it's like a mutiny in your muscle army—those fibers rebel and stubbornly stay in a shortened position, causing tension, pain, and even forcing your ankle to flex like an unwilling contortionist." Of course, John also had a dislocated knee, which can create pain as well as a sense of instability. Although the kneecap may move back into position on its own, it would certainly have been unsettling for him.

So, there was John, slight of build to begin with at 5'6" and just shy of 145 pounds, at war with the pain in his body, which was exacerbated by the elements of heat and humidity that Mother Nature was throwing at him. At some point, the realization must have sunk in for him. There would be no top-ten finish for him for this race. There would be no running to a medal or standing on a podium on this final day of the 1968 Summer Games. But even in that moment in time, when the question of stopping must have invariably arisen in his head, John ordered his body to continue.

He struggled to keep going forward, his leg heavily bandaged. At times, he slowed to a hobble, but he never stopped. He finally entered the Olympic Stadium in the darkness, well over an hour after Mamo Wolde of Ethiopia won the marathon with a time of 2:20:26. John was the fifty-seventh—and the last—of the runners to complete the 42-kilometer trek. It is common for a large cluster of marathoners to fail to finish, and that was the case in October 1968. Eighteen runners did not finish that marathon, likely as a result of some combination of injuries, fatigue, heat, or dehydration.

Although John's finishing time of 3:25:07 was not great for an elite marathoner, it still would have qualified him to run in the prestigious Boston Marathon. And, in this case, the time on the clock or the cause of the injuries were just parts of his story. More meaningful was the fact that John overcame a level of pain and physical discomfort few of us ever have to wrestle with.

So, what's so special about finishing a marathon with these sorts of injuries? First, many marathoners confronted with fatigue or heat exhaustion, let alone cramping or a dislocated knee, simply stop. On the day of John's Mexico City marathon, nearly 25 percent of the competitors did just that. Other times, marathon runners transition to walking. I can attest to having done that, blending running and walking in the several-mile-long homestretches of both marathons in which I competed. John didn't stop, and he ran virtually the whole way.

The producers of an Olympics.com video of that 1968 Mexico City marathon pondered this part of John's journey and the fortitude he displayed, training their cameras on him as he gamely soldiered through miles of pain and distress. The narrator of that video concluded that the Olympic Games provided their own special boost. "What gives these men their inner drive? What inner strength and outward pride impels them to give so much?" The narrator responded to his own queries: "The answer lies, of course, in what we call the Olympic ideal."

Perhaps John agreed that the Olympic Games spread some special sauce. After the marathon ended and John had gathered himself, he faced a group of reporters asking *why* he had chosen to keep going and finish. The man who overcame tremendous pain and fatigue overcame his limited command of the English language, too, replying eloquently, "My country did not send me 5,000 miles to *start* the race. They sent me 5,000 miles to finish the race." After he answered, John vividly recalled in our interview, he swiftly noticed a series of pens simultaneously recording the quote in notepads for posterity.

I would agree that the heroism in John's performance was that it captured the very essence of the Olympic spirit. He summoned the willpower to keep running. He overcame that desire to flip the stop switch, or to just walk the rest of the way. He likely shot down his own self-doubts. Against considerable odds, he kept going. He *finished.*

Then, upon his return to Tanzania, he was initially hailed by his countrymen. He showed me a faded newspaper article with a headline that used his middle name: "Songs for Stephen—A Big Welcome Home for Marathon Hero."

Prior to that 1968 Olympics, John had begun a six-and-a-half-year stint of military service for Tanzania as a medical assistant. Being part of the military gave him the ability to compete in marathons all over the world, something he could otherwise not have afforded. But eventually, John wanted to return to farming and his family. He showed me the documentation for his discharge in March 1972.

If there was ill will from Tanzania's military for John's decision to leave the armed forces, it was not reflected in his discharge papers. His conduct was listed as *GOOD*, and the accompanying testimonial read as follows: "Being an excellent athlete, he could not devote much time in the medical field, but his character is excellent, and [he] can be relied upon." Months later, however, any hopes John might have harbored of competing in the 1972 Summer Olympics in Munich evaporated.

"He was told to hand over his passport," Laizer said. "It was canceled. He could not go out of the country. He could not do any marathon." Laizer added that "the two things that really put him down and shattered all his dreams were when the government official took his $1,000 [prize] and when the government canceled his passport. He thought what he did, he did for his nation."

Laizer explained that although Tanzania's military leaders had helped John by affording him the opportunities and resources to build an international marathoning career, those same military leaders may have felt that John, by seeking military discharge, had stopped helping them. Moreover, Tanzania was still a young nation in 1972, intent on keeping its citizens home rather than abroad—and may not have been enamored by the idea of seeing them travel to other nations where they might be tempted by the potential lure of living elsewhere. Even now, passports are difficult to obtain from the Tanzanian government, as Laizer learned when he and his daughter endured an extremely lengthy and challenging process to secure one so she could study in the United States.

Years later, there would be some bright spots for John. He displayed a 2017 certificate from an Africa Scout Day celebration held in Arusha, where he was lauded. "In recognition of his gallantry [sic] display during the 1968 Olympic Games in Mexico finishing the marathon race despite dislocating his knee during the race." A "John Stephen Akhwari International Marathon" event was also held in June 2019, and John was a featured dignitary, handing out medals to all the participants at the half-marathon.

But in the meantime, John became disenchanted with the lack of time, attention, and resources his country put into track and field. The nation had at one time boasted track-and-field greats like Filbert Bayi and Suleiman Nyambui. Both were Olympic medal winners, and Bayi was also a former world-record holder in the 1,500 meters and the mile. That was a long time ago, and Bayi and Nyambui had become senior citizens by the time I interviewed John, who was by then also well into his eighties and needed either a cane or a wheelchair to traverse the spacious grounds of Gibb's Farm.

John was wistful about some of the ways his country had prioritized sports like soccer over his beloved track and field, and he fretted most about the message that sent to young kids. But for him, there is a difference between sadness over the state of Tanzania's athletic affairs and sadness over the state of life in his beautiful nation. Bitter would not describe him at all. He was a proud man who smiled and laughed easily and wanted to ensure we would stay for dinner at Gibb's Farm.

My wife and I, of course, did join John for dinner. Dressed nattily in suit and tie, John clearly enjoyed the chance to sample the delicious food that Gibb's Farm offered. He told us how delighted he was that his daughter Josephine connected us to him, and he invited us to someday come to his home, where he could show off all his trophies and awards. He beamed with pride as he talked about his children and his long-lasting marriage.

While there were challenges to carrying on a fluid conversation with a dinner partner who primarily spoke Swahili, we managed. It helped that the food-and-beverage manager at Gibb's Farm, Dafay Genda Umasl, came over to spend time and chat with us. As it turned out, he had known John since he was a kid, especially since the Akhwaris lived only about a kilometer away from Umasl's family in the village of Sanu Baray.

"At eight o'clock in the evening, before supper, he would get us together with the elders and talk about his story," Umasl said. Describing the stories John would tell regarding the 1968 marathon, he added, "As kids, we loved him, because after he had fallen down . . . we couldn't understand why he didn't go to the car." He said the kids in the village were always amazed by John's "ambition to finish, and not to end [it] in the middle."

During our interview, and again at dinner, John brought with him green lanyards tied around medals, like the ones he had given out for the half-marathon over which he presided in 2019. He presented me with one during the interview and my wife with one during dinner, eagerly ensuring we took photos with him and displayed the shiny medals. Fittingly, each medal was inscribed with the same quote John provided to reporters following that 1968 marathon run and their question as to why he persevered: "My country did not send me 5,000 miles to start the race. They sent me 5,000 miles to finish the race."

After dinner, we helped the Gibb's Farm staff wheel John back to his room. We said a temporary goodbye, knowing we would see this man once more the following morning. As we headed to breakfast the next day, Umasl informed us that after we had retired for the evening, John had returned to the dining room and bar. He had regaled several other American visitors with his story, given medals to them, and let them know that a Seattle-area writer was at the farm and would be writing a book detailing his courageous marathon finish back in 1968. We ended up talking with several of these Americans, most visiting from the San Francisco Bay Area. We got a charge out of the fact that John had laughed with, talked with, and touched so many in such a short period of time.

An hour or so later, we packed up to prepare for the next leg of our Tanzania trip, one that would feature several safaris through the massive and majestic Serengeti National Park. We walked out to the Gibb's Farm lobby and the oval turnabout at the front of the hotel where vehicles did drop-offs and pickups. John was there, in good spirits, to greet us.

As we waited with him for the motorcycle rider who would take him on the first leg of his trip home, he suddenly called Teri over to him. It was clear he liked her a lot—not a surprise, since virtually everyone does. "When you get back home," he said to Teri, with me in earshot, "don't forget me."

Mr. Akhwari, I don't see how we ever could.

PART II

OVERCOMING MEDICAL AND PSYCHOLOGICAL CHALLENGES

CHAPTER 5

WILLIAM AND CHARLES FLAHERTY, COMMONWEALTH OF PUERTO RICO

ALPINE SKIING, 2018 WINTER OLYMPICS, PYEONGCHANG (CHARLES), AND 2022 WINTER OLYMPICS, BEIJING (WILLIAM)

On the Caribbean Sea, about one thousand miles southeast of Miami, lies the Commonwealth of Puerto Rico. It's a territory that serves up a near-constant diet of eighty-degree-plus days to its over three million residents. Not the sort of place you would point to as a haven for alpine skiing—any more than those who haven't watched *Cool Runnings* would picture Jamaica as an Olympic bobsledding country.

As unlikely as it may seem, Charles and William Flaherty carved out a place in the annals of Olympic skiing for Puerto Rico. But the challenges Charles and William overcame to clip into a pair of skis at a Winter Olympics almost pale in comparison to the ones that they and their mother, Ann Flaherty, have stared down over the years.

Years ago, medical percentages told Ann and her husband, Dennis, that their youngest son, William, might not live to this day—yet he has. The Flahertys didn't figure that their oldest son would play a central role in saving his younger brother, but Charles surely did. And they wouldn't have believed that Dennis, the husband and father who was equal parts inspiration, guiding light, and mentor to his family, would pass away suddenly in 2018 at age forty-eight. Through it all, the Flaherty family has survived—even thrived.

"People tell me I've been to hell and back," William said matter-of-factly, "but for me, it's just my life."

To tell the story of that life and trace the journey of this incredible family, we need to jump back a little over a decade and a half to 2008. Cincinnati, Ohio, was the place the Flahertys called home. It was where Charles was born in December of 2000 and where William was born in May of 2004. It was also where, in 2008, the family received the devastating news that William was suffering from a disease called hemophagocytic lymphohistiocytosis (HLH) and needed a transplant to save his life.

Antonio Colón, close friend of the family's and former associate of Dennis's, tells the story of doctors first diagnosing William's condition and concluding it was either HLH or cancer. The doctors told them to "pray for cancer," said Colón, who later became head of the Puerto Rican Federation of Winter Athletes.

There was good reason for the doctors' fear of HLH. It is an uncommon and life-threatening blood disorder that typically manifests in children before they reach the age of one. When the disease strikes, there is an uncontrolled proliferation of white blood cells called lymphocytes and immune-system cells called macrophages. The overactive immune system in a patient with HLH is essentially on fire and under assault. By attacking its own organs, the body ultimately kills itself. HLH can initially show up as a fever, an enlargement of the liver and spleen, enlarged lymph nodes, a rash, or yellow discoloration of the skin and eyes, which was the condition Ann noticed in William.

To prolong his life, a bone-marrow transplant was necessary, and there happened to be a perfect match: his older brother. But helping seven-year-old Charles understand the intricacies of such a surgery was no small feat. Colón, on the receiving end of intimate stories Dennis shared with him about the surgery, recalled that at first, Charles was hesitant, harboring a perception that the transplant might harm him.

Ann said what Charles recalls is asking her and Dennis whether they would "still like him when he was a bag of Jell-O because he was giving away his bones."

For Ann, the memories of that time are filled with distinct recollections of just how dire the outlook was for William, especially in the months between entering Cincinnati Children's Hospital in early 2008 and when the transplant occurred in April. "There were days when we didn't know if he was going to live through the next twenty-four hours," Ann said. "I remember a day [when] he was just lying in my arms, like a dead weight, flaccid. That feeling of having your child almost lifeless in your arms, you don't forget that."

Loved ones and friends encouraged Ann to go to the gym and get away a bit for her own well-being during those rough months. But she couldn't run more than a lap or two without a morbid fear of what she would do if something happened to William while she was exercising. Even stopping for gas en route to the hospital—and the extra five minutes of time that would take away from seeing William—terrified her.

As it was, the shoulders Ann and her family were able to lean on, literally and figuratively, were lifesavers. Medical professionals like Dr. Jack Bleesing and Dr. Nada Yazigi, whom Ann credited with zeroing in on William's HLH diagnosis, were of course instrumental. So were those around the family. "I'm forever indebted to the people of Cincinnati," she said.

In the hospital, the Flahertys were showered with kindness. Ann remembered the first day William received chemotherapy, which was considered an effective way to neutralize HLH, even though it isn't cancer per se. "Someone brought me a dinner at the hospital. I cried on that stranger's shoulder, and I didn't even know who she was." At the same time, they reached out to others who needed their empathy just as much as their son did. Ann recalled comforting "a young man next door who was on his third transplant and was from Florida, and he didn't have anyone."

During this time of urgent need, Ann's husband looked for the sunshine within each day. Dennis "was good about keeping a positive attitude. He didn't let anyone play the 'poor me' card, and he ensured we laughed every day." She also had a mom who, despite her own medical battles, saw an upside to their ongoing struggles. "My mother used to call us the luckiest unlucky people ever. We had amazing doctors, a perfect match for a bone-marrow donor, great insurance, and a community of friends."

In the end, the April 2008 surgery was a success. It was more of an ordeal for Charles, because the surgery to harvest the bone marrow from his hips took two and a half hours in the operating room. For William, the procedure was simpler. "Nurses hooked up the bag of marrow to his IV pole, attached it to his central line, and let it roll into his blood stream. Once in the blood stream, the marrow knew where to go on its own," Ann said.

While the transplant procedure for William was simple, being an HLH survivor has been anything but. The transplant would be among the earliest of more than twenty surgeries he has endured, along with postsurgery chemotherapy and at least seventy-five blood transfusions. Ann said that about every two years, some type of medical complication has arisen for her younger son.

To push past William's medical challenges, and certainly in the aftermath of the transplant, the Flahertys have used the medicine of humor and laughter. Ann joked that it took only about twenty-four hours after the surgery for her boys to start bickering again. William cracked that, posttransplant, "Charles tried to pull out the 'I just saved your life' card, but I'm not gonna lie, I just don't suck up to him." Charles said of that time, "I was in first grade, and now I realize I've been through the ringer. But back then, I think I was more worried about what I was going to have for lunch, or what to do when I got on the playground."

In the chaotic months after the transplant, doctors and psychologists advised Ann that keeping her boys active would be key. Activities and adventures served as saviors for the entire Flaherty family as they all embraced the see-the-positives outlook that Dennis subscribed to, and viewed their lives as a series of opportunities rather than dwelling on setbacks.

"We very rarely say no to adventure," Ann said, citing a trip she, Dennis, and her sons took that they referred to as the Flahertys' very own "Around the World in Eighty Days." Their itinerary included stops in Hawaii, New Zealand, Australia, Singapore, Hong Kong, Thailand, India, Dubai, China, Zimbabwe, South Africa, and more.

Charles Flaherty flashes a smile after his performance representing Puerto Rico at the 2018 Winter Games. Credit: Antonio Colon

Charles summed it up this way: "We get bored and start doing crazy things."

William added, "Our philosophy is that you always take the more exciting [or] fun option." And one of the options they decided to pursue following William's transplant was skiing.

To the outside viewer, skiing might not seem the safest activity for young kids, particularly one who has been through a lifesaving bone-marrow transplant. But Ann was never worried about skiing being dangerous. She and her husband had competitive sporting in their genes: Dennis had been on the rowing team at Northeastern University and Ann had been on the sailing team at Boston College. They both also skied, and doctors had indicated that skiing could deliver the added benefit of strengthening William's bone density.

The Flahertys pursued skiing at a high level, even after moving to a sun-worshipping territory in the Caribbean. In 2010, the family relocated to Puerto Rico when Dennis landed an opportunity to grow his business there and after Ann, who has a background in nursing, consulted William's medical team.

Ann wanted to ensure the superb medical care William had received at Cincinnati Children's could be replicated. She also wanted to address her concern that bone-marrow transplant patients could be especially susceptible to sunburns. Dr. Bleesing, knowing the family would return to Cincinnati for occasional check-in appointments, gave them the green light. "Go, get out of here. It might end up being the best thing for you." It didn't hurt that the family found a top-level, Johns Hopkins University–trained pediatrician in Puerto Rico.

So the family seized the chance to start a new chapter in life and to soak up the rays on a tropical island. "I still miss Cincinnati—I miss the people," Ann said. "But it's more fun to be by the ocean." After the Flahertys moved, Ann figured her boys would grow up to be sailing or surfing aficionados. But the family had routinely gone on ski vacations in Colorado, and that didn't change. At first, William wasn't able to travel on those vacations, but in 2010, all four of the Flahertys trekked to Colorado, and both boys had a fabulous time.

The trips continued in 2011, 2012, and 2013, and the notion of taking Charles's and William's skiing talents up a notch came when they were paired with a ski instructor named Mike Williams. When Williams suggested getting the boys into ski racing, it seemed like a perfect marriage of two goal-oriented boys with an instructor who loved to teach.

Williams, who was in his midsixties at the time, had begun skiing at age four, a byproduct of having a best friend whose parents were ski instructors. In 1960, he became good enough to try out for a national team. He went to Michigan, taught his first ski class on a blue-sky afternoon, and "was smitten" with teaching others, he said. He eventually found his way to Beaver Creek, Colorado, where he met the Flaherty boys and encouraged them to see skiing as more than just family adventures on trails and through woods. "They were both good skiers to start with—and you know, at that age, kids have no fear," Williams said.

Charles began to excel, finishing first in his age group at an EpicMix Racing event when he was thirteen. Lindsey Vonn had been brought in as a celebrity skier and pacesetter, and after the race, Charles had his photo snapped with the three-time Olympic medal winner.

Meanwhile, William wanted to emulate his older brother. "It's safe to say that [Charles] really showed me it was possible," William said. Charles was reaching new heights with the help of a coach named Sara Radamus, an inductee into the Middlebury Athletics Hall of Fame in Vermont for both her skiing and tennis prowess. She eventually became instrumental in William's skiing journey as well, serving as his personal coach in his last year of ski racing.

Both boys recalled 2014 to 2015 as the timeframe for when they made the transition from skiing well to barreling down the slopes in pursuit of a bigger end game. As they advanced, William raced around Colorado, and Charles stepped up to race nationwide. And Dennis, highly successful in his business and immersed in philanthropy in the San Juan area, began to pursue the idea of reawakening Puerto Rico's Olympic winter-sports program.

It's difficult to pinpoint exactly why a tropical-island commonwealth ever wanted to field a Winter Olympics team in the first place, although Puerto Ricans take great pride in playing and excelling in competitive sports. In fact, Puerto Rico had previously experienced a brief tenure in the Olympic Winter Games, fielding teams in the 1984, 1988, 1992, 1994, and 1998 Winter Games. Then came a 2002 snafu in Salt Lake City, which aborted the winter program. After the Puerto Rican athletes marched in the opening ceremonies, all set to enter the bobsled competition, they had to withdraw after it was determined that one of the athletes failed to meet Puerto Rico Olympic Committee eligibility guidelines.

Now, Dennis dreamed of resuscitating Puerto Rico's winter sports and having his boys ski for the commonwealth in the Winter Olympics. But he and Ann knew the job of rekindling a winter-sports program needed to be much bigger and broader than just promoting his two kids, so he tapped into a local business associate he could trust. Colón, an accountant by trade, had a thirst for the challenge that Dennis was taking on. After all, he had already navigated a professional career involving everything from constructing a building to helping produce a movie. "It's kind of crazy—but that's who I am," Colón said.

In working to restart the winter-sports federation, the Flahertys and Colón encountered an anxious, if not fully resistant, commonwealth. Ann said the officials in Puerto Rico "were very cautious" and needed to know there would be a sustained commitment to the program. "I *do* remember someone saying that it was not just going to be a one-and-done." She also recalled that the reactions to the reestablishing of a Puerto Rican winter team, and the involvement of her kids in stoking that dream, ran the gamut. "Some people laughed," she said, "and others would take it very seriously." Colón said that, until Dennis came along, nobody else had devised a comprehensive plan. But Dennis, who was determined that the effort be done well and done right, understood the program had to transcend the limits of just a couple of athletes.

Brett Borgard, another ski coach who worked with the Flaherty boys—particularly William—agreed that Dennis had a strong ambition to do this. But without the commitment of the boys, the Olympic dream could not possibly have come together. "Their ambition was eye opening. They would ski year-round. They went to Whistler, to Chile, anywhere they could—and with a smile on their faces." He added that it was amazing they could keep up with their grades and their lifestyle. "They set a goal, and they achieved it." Although Charles and William benefited from having parents with resources, they worked extremely hard to get better at skiing while keeping up with schoolwork. Colón emphasized that they trained like professional athletes for five to six hours every day and then went home to do their homework.

With the kids invested in getting better on the slopes, with Dennis both emotionally and financially committed to establishing a Winter Olympics team, and with the federation structure that Colón and others put in place, the buildup finally began.

One thing that helped Puerto Rico restart the program was that the guidelines enabling athletes to qualify for the Olympic team were flexible. Athletes could do so if they either were born in the commonwealth, were second-generation born, or had resided in Puerto Rico for more than thirty-six months. By the time Charles and William competed in the Winter Games, they had been residents of Puerto Rico for eight and twelve years, respectively.

In anticipation of the 2018 Olympic Winter Games, the boys started a training program that would take them to the mountains of major United States ski resorts for several months at a time. They combined that with an academic regimen of classes through an accredited online institution. Both boys earned straight As and remain excellent students. After Charles made the national team, he needed to qualify for the Winter Games. This involved meeting a complicated points threshold, established by the International Ski and Snowboard Federation, based on where the skier placed in a series of qualifying races. For the 2018 giant slalom, Charles needed to be below 140 points, and when he qualified in December 2017, it was game on. "We went from 0 to 100 in no time," Colón said.

He and the Flaherty family experienced the pomp, the circumstance, and the incredible majesty that comes with being in an Olympic competition, and Charles carried the Puerto Rican flag for the opening ceremonies in Pyeongchang. "The whole Olympic movement is beautiful—the closest thing to the perfect world," Colón said. "There is this sense of camaraderie, and you see how [the athletes] take care of each other."

Charles recalled the eyes of the world on him and the other competitors. "We had world leaders with us, and the vice president of the United States watched us," he said. Ann added, "It's hard to put into words. I was screaming obnoxiously. You could hear me through the TV! You can hear it when Charles did his second run, and you watch the videos. I was just so proud. It's a great accomplishment, and I am incredibly proud of them for sticking with it."

Charles ended up placing seventy-third out of the hundred and ten skiers who entered the giant slalom course and the seventy-five skiers who completed it.

As the 2018 Games drew to a close, Ann said Charles's experience fueled his little brother's ambitions. She said that William declared, "I kind of want to do it, too." In fact, William said, he had begun harboring his own Olympic dreams for a few years by then. With that, the younger brother threw himself into preparation for the forthcoming 2022 Winter Games in Beijing, which was to be held less than fifteen years after his lifesaving surgery.

What made William's journey all the more remarkable was that HLH compromised about a third of his immune system. When a routine sickness came along, it could take him up to two weeks to recover and get back to normal, compared to one to two days for many others. But that was where he, and everyone else in the family, forcefully shut down the pity party. "I could sit and mope, but I really don't see the point," William said. "As things come up, you adjust to them."

"The tenacity of that kid was amazing," added Borgard, recalling a young athlete who "knew all the big doctor words" and was regularly "defying a lot of odds." He spent a lot of time with William, both on and off the ski hills, noting how William "never talked negatively about anybody. He was very goal-oriented, and he was wanting to know about you as a person. There was this desire to learn and improve. Both boys fit into that category because that's what their mom and dad instilled in them."

As his brother had done before him, William met the Puerto Rican and international standards for entry into the 2022 Games in Beijing. He went one better than his older brother by qualifying for two events: slalom, where he finished forty-fourth, and giant slalom, where he came in fortieth. Charles had, as he said, finished just "five lousy points" from qualifying for the slalom in 2018.

Colón felt that William may have placed better than Charles because he didn't have to deal with the pressure of being on the *first* Puerto Rican team in the renewed Winter Olympics program. His optimistic outlook helped him, too, stated Colón. "He said, 'I'm here, and I'm enjoying it.' Every day of the Olympics, he had the biggest smile and was having the time of his life."

Either way, William carried the Puerto Rican flag into the 2022 Winter Games opening ceremonies, describing it this way: "You walk out of this tunnel and under these suspended [Olympic] rings, and it's like, *Holy crap, I'm here.* It really hit me then. It really is something bigger than your achievements."

Dennis was not there to see that story unfold or to witness William's performance firsthand, but Ann had little doubt he would have been every bit as vocal, every bit as proud, and every bit as touched as she was, for both their boys. "You wouldn't have been able to shut him up," she joked. "He would have been shouting from the rooftops."

Yet while the Flaherty boys' journey through trails of illness, grief, and competitive skiing generated a lot of compassion, positive applause, and praise, their path was not easy. They and their family also encountered skepticism, second glances, and probing questions.

As a young boy, Charles dealt with being shunned and verbally hazed by other boys when he first began to ski competitively, having taken up the sport at a later age than many peers who had been skiing since they were six years old. "I came in when I was thirteen," he explained, "and I wasn't very socially aware." He became the easy target to yell at, to cast aside, and to isolate; he was the introverted kid who wasn't invited to social events and birthday parties. Charles responded to the bullying by pushing back with training and skill. "I started beating people in races," he said, and some of the kids who had mistreated him eventually came around. One even offered a formal apology, "which was pretty rewarding."

As a teen, William experienced some of the ugliness of critics and whisperers who unleash venom from the anonymity of their computer keyboards. When he announced on Instagram that he was going to the Olympics, he received a lot of supportive responses but also some from trolls and haters who blasted him.

Then there were the members of the media, who have not been above tossing harsh questions at even the most gifted of athletes. As the first of the brothers to compete for Puerto Rico, Charles bore the brunt of questions about whether he was in the Olympic Games due to talent or due to the circumstances of being on a fledgling Winter Games team. Charles had qualified fair and square, but it was true that he and his brother would have had a much more intense challenge in making a US team, which limited the number of qualifiers in each event.

"Listen, I qualified under the Olympic standard, and I qualified under Puerto Rico's standard," Charles said to interviewers. "If you have a problem with any of that, that's where your issues are." Of the media who were critical, Charles said pointedly, "They didn't get up at three thirty in the morning and freeze their asses on a chairlift for twelve hours."

Williams, the Flaherty boys' first coach, said the brothers achieved, and surpassed, their goals of finishing and of not being last in their Olympic competitions. Charles started out at a hundred and fifth in the giant slalom and rose to seventy-third place, while William started eighty-ninth and finished in the middle of the pack. Moreover, Williams stressed that the boys carried the flag, served as standard-bearers, and competed at a level most never will. "It's hours and hours on the hill. It's

William Flaherty poses, marking his fifteenth year of surviving organ transplant surgery in 2008. Credit: Ann E. Flaherty

fitness training. It's day-in and day-out attention to diet. It's dedicating themselves not just to athletic training but to educational training and being top students. Neither one has to apologize for where they got and how they did it. I would challenge anyone to compete with those boys, because they couldn't do it."

Beyond the slopes, Charles and William seem to have grown up to be extremely talented at the game of *life*, thanks in large part to the parents who modeled positive attitudes and values daily. Ann remembered Dennis as an intense powerhouse who spread lots of laughs. William remembered that his father taught his sons the importance of staying on task and finishing. There was, additionally, an ethos of giving within the Flaherty household, and one of Dennis's legacies involved helping to establish the HLH Center of Excellence at Cincinnati Children's Hospital. Those efforts helped lead, among other things, to the Food and Drug Administration approval of a treatment drug for the disease that had ravaged William.

The unsung hero of the family, though, may well be Ann, who held the household together, took Charles and William to all their skiing events, and endured the same three-thirty morning wake-up call as her boys did.

As for the kids, Colón has thought of Charles as a visionary and expects "something really big to come out of that kid." Indeed, Charles graduated in December 2023 from Embry-Riddle Aeronautical University with a degree in mechanical engineering and a focus on propulsion. Having previously earned three internships with SpaceX in Brownsville, Texas, he helped design and build rocket launchpads, and he went to full-time status with the corporation in February 2024 to join a team responsible for the daily operation and maintenance of a rocket called Starship. He is now both an Olympian and a rocket scientist. "When I log in," he shared, "it says 'Commander Flaherty.'"

William, an aerospace-engineering major at Purdue University, twice received the "Character Award" from Ski and Snowboard Club Vail and also received the club's "Commitment Award" once. That is emblematic of the upbeat attitude he exhibited over the years, from working to near exhaustion on the slopes to bringing his own waffle maker to ski camp to make waffles for the other kids. Borgard praised his tenacity, his humility, and his desire to positively impact others.

William's competitive skiing career ended after a 2022 surgery, where doctors removed a bone from one of his legs to rebuild a section of his jaw—which they believed had been damaged by the chemotherapy and steroids used to save his life. Regardless, Colón believes that William's life experience is going to translate into "something very special for humanity."

As a family, the Flahertys have sought to put their Olympic

experience into perspective. It was memorable, but they did not see it as their defining moment. Charles joked about how mentioning to people that he made an Olympic appearance and has a Wikipedia page is "one of my party tricks." William admitted that not even his college roommate knew he was an Olympian. Ann said she gets in trouble with her boys "if I tell people my kids are Olympians." Ann quickly added, though, that having had an Olympic experience will always be with her sons.

And of course, there is a beautiful thing that sprouted from their experience—the sustaining of momentum for the winter-sports program the Flahertys rekindled. In the 2018 Winter Olympics, Charles was the sole representative of Puerto Rico, and in 2022, William was one of two on the commonwealth's Winter Games team. But plans for future Winter Olympics include athletes who will compete in luge, men's and women's skiing, ice hockey, and curling. This will be much more than a one-off. "The Flaherty dream became a reality, and out of that, it became a legacy," Colón said.

The Flaherty boys and their parents put their time in, and the reward was to have a reawakened Puerto Rican Winter Olympics program represented by young men who overcame every single obstacle before them. "These are two special human beings," Borgard said of William and Charles. "They're not like 99 percent of the kids out there. We're speaking about kids who did amazing things and are still doing amazing things. You want to follow their story."

CHAPTER 6

—————

BRIAN STEMMLE, CANADA

ALPINE SKIING, 1998 WINTER OLYMPICS, NAGANO

Over a quarter century later, the rivers of emotion wash over Brian Stemmle's face, crack his voice, transform his whole being. It is as if he has been teleported back to 1998, to Japan, to his fourth appearance in the Winter Olympics.

Brian had fervently believed his final trip to the Winter Games would be a triumphant one. He had a secret weapon—a sign in his pocket, a premonition that could only lead to one successful result. As we chatted over Zoom, he screen-shared an article titled "Nagano Gold" that he had clipped out of a newspaper six months before he competed in the alpine skiing downhill and super G events in those 1998 Games. That faded article had been Brian's rabbit's foot.

"It went in my left pocket," he said, choking up at the memory. "Whatever I was wearing each day, it was in my pocket. Every time I put my hand in my pocket, I thought of my coaches watching me." At night, the thoughts resumed. "Every time I went to bed, I thought of the course. Every kind of scenario you could imagine—I thought of it."

There had been three other Winter Olympics for this sublime skier, but they hadn't gone Brian's way. February 13, 1998, would be different. "I wanted to be at my best and not let anything stop me," he said.

It is excruciating to think of just how close Brian was to fulfilling his vision. It is much more excruciating to consider how close he came to perishing nearly a decade earlier, on one of the most dangerous downhill courses in the world. He has stared down death and family tragedy and disappointment, but he has come out the other side. Although his saga is tinged by misfortune, it is also laden with multiple helpings of resilience, perseverance, and willpower.

Brian Stemmle's life story began on October 12, 1966, in Aurora, a community in the Canadian province of Ontario that lies about forty-five kilometers (twenty-eight miles) north of Toronto. It seemed preordained that Brian and his older sister, Karen, would have skis on their feet and poles in their hands. Their dad, Wilf, an avid skier, had immigrated to Toronto from Germany at age thirteen and had taken their mom, Andrea, to a ski lodge for their first date. He later recruited her to team up with him on the Blue Mountain Ski Patrol so they could ski for free. After they convinced Brian and Karen's grandparents to relocate to the shores of Georgian Bay, the family had a place to stay every weekend, and the kids had weekly access to Georgian Peaks. A scenic private ski facility above Georgian Bay, it boasted the highest vertical drop of any resort in Ontario.

Before long, Brian and his sister were on a ski team with friends, schussing down the mountains and building a reputation as "always the last ones off the hill," he said. An athlete for all seasons, Brian joked that he became a good figure skater "until I was teased in high school." He also played soccer, quarterbacked the high school football team, windsurfed, mountain biked, and played baseball and hockey. But when he was about fourteen and had to choose between skiing and hockey, the sport with the powder aced out the one with the ice.

Brian said the prowess of a sister who was two and a half years older helped make that choice easier. "She was always on a [ski] team in front of me," he said, adding that Karen subsequently made the national development team and then the Canadian National Team.

"Brian always tried to keep up with me," Karen said. "I just

One of Brian Stemmle's coaches said that, in his prime, he was the best ski jumper on the World Cup circuit. Here he is, airborne, in 1991. Credit: © Malcolm Carmichael

remember him being so competitive." The finish-first mentality flashed with skiing, ski jumping, racing back to a water-ski dock, virtually any activity—and Karen said it hasn't subsided much. She called him a special breed and recounted a story from a past Christmas when her husband and his family rented a curling rink, long before curling became an Olympic sport. "Brian gets on the ice, and he's talking to his team and yelling, 'Hurry, hurry hard!' So, I said, 'Brian, how many times have you done this?' And he said, 'None—it's my first time.'" In poking fun at her younger brother, she also revealed a gift of his: the ability to observe just about any athletic activity and perform it well the very first time. "His visualization skills are just excellent," she said.

Brian didn't visualize himself as an elite skier to begin with. "For me, it was always being good and having fun. I don't know if I was great." The lure of skiing for Brian "was the fun factor. Flying through the air was just the most exhilarating thing."

His sister agreed. "I always say we got good by accident. It was so raw and organic and innocent. We had no thought of the Olympics."

Still, bit by bit, the Olympics crossed onto their radar as the kids advanced from the Georgian Peaks ski team to the Southern Ontario team to the Ontario team. It wasn't long before they were ready for the national team, along with most of Canada's other proficient skiers who hailed from Ontario, British Columbia, Alberta, and Quebec.

It was Karen who first burst the Olympic Games bubble. She finished fourth in a World Cup race in Switzerland, took twenty-second place in the downhill in the 1984 Winter Olympics in Sarajevo, and spent five years on the Canadian National Team. But there would be no second Olympic appearance for her. She failed to make Canada's 1988 women's team, achieving nine objectives the Canadian coaches laid out for her, but falling short of a tenth that required a finish in the top twenty of two World Cup races.

That left Karen in tears at the time, but she was later able to diffuse the narrow miss with humor. Brian cracked, "She always says, 'Between my brother and I, we've been in five Olympics.'"

Inspired by her success, Brian became a mainstay on the Canadian men's national team, if not one of its brightest lights. He was one of the stars of the Canadian team when Benoit "Benny" Lalande came along as an assistant coach. They had a bit of a rough start when, during a summer camp for the ski team, Lalande pulled a practical joke by turning his truck in front of Brian's car to prevent him from getting out of the parking lot. Brian didn't see the humor, and the young coach realized he may not have selected the best time to tweak Brian's funny bone. "Here I'm the rookie coach, dinking around with the big star of the team," Lalande said.

They both got over it, and the assistant coach developed a deep admiration for his ski-team standout. "He was a very, very good athlete—and very smooth," Lalande said. As he got to know Brian better, he, like Karen, observed that there was seemingly no sport Brian couldn't conquer. Backflips off the diving board. Volleyball. Golf. And on the slopes—especially with his jumps—he was a picture of near perfection.

"In his prime, he was the best jumper of the World Cup [circuit] for sure," Lalande said. "Other teams would take video of him. He was so smooth, so technically perfect. You didn't really have to teach him." And in virtually every race he entered, Brian was a contender to win. In fact, if the coaches were surprised at anything, it was that Brian didn't win *more* often.

Yet Brian won plenty, excelling enough to make the team for the 1988 Winter Games in Calgary. It was his first Olympics, a "happy to be here" sort of moment. When he ended up being disqualified from the alpine skiing downhill because he missed a gate, he knew he would have more opportunities. What he most lamented was that he had missed a "once in a lifetime" chance to medal at a Winter Olympics on Canadian soil.

In 1988 and throughout his career, there was one particular opponent Brian faced routinely—one that undercut him just as much as icy snow, narrow gates, tight turns, and competitors: injuries. Brian said he'd experienced "nothing crazy" in terms of spills or wounds when he was a younger skier. But then, on an outing to Georgian Peaks at age seventeen, he broke a ski pole before attempting a jump and punctured a forearm, injured a muscle, and left a six-inch scar on the inside of his left arm. He spent New Year's Eve in a hospital bed.

There were other injuries, too, but Brian shrugged them off the way most of us would downplay a headache or an aching muscle. For example, he went ahead and competed in Calgary in 1988 just one month after suffering a torn anterior cruciate ligament (ACL) injury, wearing a brace and managing his way through the stiffness. He said skiers must very commonly overcome ACL tears the same way basketball players frequently deal with sprained ankles and base-ball pitchers overcome Tommy John surgery to the ligaments inside their elbows. "For a skier, an ACL injury is like a cavity for any other kid," Brian said. "I saw it as a blip in the road. I still had that sense of invincibility."

Even as the physical setbacks mounted, Brian kept his ski tips and his career pointed up. But an eerie trend was beginning to form—one he wouldn't discover until he had done some after-the-fact research on his career. It turns out he was especially prone to injury on one particular day.

"January 14 was not good for me," he said.

It all began on that day in 1987, when a ski came off and he tore his patellar tendon during a race in Germany. Exactly a year later, in Austria, it was a torn ACL. But those setbacks were mere child's play compared to what happened on January 14, 1989. That day, Brian stood atop Mount Hahnenkamm in Kitzbühel, 5,610 feet above sea level in the Austrian Alps. It was a World Cup competition in a place that is legendary among those in the sport. "Kitzbühel is like the Super Bowl of skiing," Brian said.

The run Brian would be going down was called the Steilhang, part of the Streif racecourse. Austria's official travel site, Austria.info, de-scribed the mountain, the course, and the run this way: "The name alone is enough to raise the hairs on some athletes' backs. Each year in mid-January, the Hahnenkamm downhill race in Kitzbühel takes place on one of the most dangerous ski runs in the world. With a gra-dient of up to 85 percent and top speeds of ninety miles (145 km) per hour, even the most experienced skiers will feel a rush of adrenaline on the Streif."

For context, that 85 percent gradient at the top of the run is the kind of steep drop found on only a handful of ski mountains in the world. Brian, then twenty-two and a rising star on the Canadian team, probably viewed the race as a life-changing event. It was—in a more tragic way than he could ever have imagined.

Ominously, before Brian began his run, Canadian coaches had noticed a serious flaw with the netting adjacent to the Steilhang run.

Unlike most other parts of the ski hill, it lacked plastic coating around the fencing. Canada's coaches asked that race organizers add more, but apparently there was no more material available at that time. That meant ski racers could more easily get stuck in the fencing if they encountered it.

Did the coaches mention anything to their skiers about the lack of plastic? Absolutely not, Brian later said. "There was no talk about it; it was only afterward that I realized. I'm thinking, *I'm not going to make a mistake—I've gone over it [in my mind] a million times.'* Plus, the last thing out of a coach's mouth is to say, 'Be careful.'"

Those in the know say the Steilhang run demands near-perfect precision. Its curves force skiers to the outside of the hill, which is closest to the fencing, just after they have navigated the steepest section of it. Racers must exhibit nerveless control at high speeds and sharp angles. Brian approached, knowing he needed to extend his left ski, plant, and make a hairpin right turn.

"When I made the left-foot turn, I really thought I'd pull it off," he said. "The last thing I remember was seeing my ski tip go into the net. I didn't realize I'd caught my pole, and that's what spun me around." He got stuck in the fencing, with horrific results.

Brian's race was over, and for harrowing days and weeks, there was considerable worry that his life was, too.

Karen recalled sharing her angst with coworkers on Friday the thirteenth. "I remember telling people I was nervous, because Brian was racing Kitzbühel." The next morning, at 6:30 a.m. local time on the fourteenth, the phone rang at Karen's home. It was one of the Canadian team officials. "It was the coach, telling me Brian got hurt. When he said internal injuries and a broken pelvis, I didn't understand. I hung up the phone, and I was dumbfounded. I didn't understand how bad it was." Still, she quickly phoned the ski club, knowing her dad had planned to be skiing there that weekend, and she told workers there to get her father right away.

Brian described his next two weeks in an Innsbruck hospital as among the most painful in his life, as if he were being perpetually kicked in the groin. He dealt with a life-threatening blend of physical challenges, including the broken pelvis, massive internal injuries, intensive swelling, and infections. With tubes connected to various parts of his body, Brian was put into a medically induced coma and underwent twenty-five blood transfusions.

Karen said the doctors opined at one point that her brother had a 50 percent chance to live. She said those same doctors credited Brian's age, his level of fitness, and drugs for saving his life. A sweet coincidence, Karen said, is that the first day Brian awakened and learned he would make it was his dad's birthday.

Brian emerged from the hospital alive, albeit a physical wreck. So now what? After nearly dying on a mountain, could he even entertain the thought of skiing down other ones?

His older sister knew what *her* answer would have been had she been in her brother's shoes. During our Zoom interview, Karen dramatically slashed her hand across her throat to emphasize the "no way" conclusion she would have come to. A ski mountain had just delivered a near-fatal blow to her younger brother. So how in the world could he stay in the sport?

"Nobody thought of him skiing—his pelvis was wired back together," she said. "Forget the physical part. The mental side of throwing yourself down a hill at ninety miles per hour . . . I've just always admired that Brian could do it."

Brian said his parents, who had stood beside his hospital bed just hoping he would remain alive, were not excited by the prospect of their son returning to ski racing. But his thought process was dominated by his competitive streak. "I just never want to be defeated by anything, especially a mountain. I wanted to try and be a ski racer again . . . There was not any doubt in my mind, ever, once the pain went away."

He had a long road to recovery before that would happen, which included undergoing a colostomy, wearing a special bag on his stomach for three months, and losing forty-five pounds. And there were a couple of additional hard tasks ahead of him. One involved following the advice of his agents to file suit against those who operated the ski mountain and ran the Kitzbühel event.

"I was really hesitant about suing someone in the [ski] community," Brian said. But his decision was spurred by a desire "to make it safer for the other racers. There was never really any money in it." That decision was validated in 1991, when a promising Austrian downhill skier named Gernot Reinstadler died on a different mountain under similar circumstances. Reinstadler, only twenty, lost control during a training run for what was called the Lauberhorn race, crashing into safety nets at full speed and trapping one of his skis in them. He suffered a pelvic fracture, severe internal injuries, and bleeding. The legal process for Brian's case took a few years to unwind, but in the end, it culminated in a decision in his favor by Austria's Supreme Court.

Brian's second difficult task was to engage in "tough conversations" with his mom and dad. "I wanted to let them know if I could try, I would. And that I would take [the] right steps and dedicate myself to being a better athlete." His parents may not have liked his decision, but Brian said they did not stand in the way of it or attempt to tell him what to do.

What came next was astonishing, given the severity of his internal injuries. He went back to skiing at an elite level and won the Winter Pan American Games in Argentina in 1990. He competed on the Canadian Alpine Skiing teams in the 1992 Winter Olympics in France, finishing twenty-third in the downhill. And, in the 1994 Winter Games in Lillehammer, he finished twenty-sixth in the super G.

But Brian felt there was more to do. He thought back to his first three experiences in the Olympics with a palpable level of frustration. Calgary 1988: just months after his recovery from the torn ACL, he "went out like a Mack Truck" and didn't retain enough strength in his legs to finish. Albertville 1992: he tore both rotator cuffs and couldn't lift his arms above his shoulders. Lillehammer 1994: he failed to focus on his own race and his own technique. "I was trying to ski like everybody else," he said.

Brian needed something more to get him to that next level, and the one person who could help him attain that goal was Dr. Dana Sinclair, who became the performance psychologist for Brian and the rest of the Canadian men's and women's Alpine Skiing teams.

A licensed psychologist with doctorates from both the University of Cambridge and the University of Ottawa, Dr. Sinclair has worked with thousands of Olympic and other athletes, including professionals from the National Football League (NFL), Major League Baseball (MLB), the National Basketball Association (NBA), the National Hockey League (NHL), the Women's Tennis Association (WTA), the Professional Golfers' Association (PGA), and the IndyCar Series. On this long list of athletes, Brian ranked near the top. "He is obviously one of my all-time favorites," Dr. Sinclair said. "I admire him tremendously for what he did and how he did it." Asked to sum up Brian, she didn't hesitate. "Tough. Calm. Composed. He's fun, too."

One of the earliest and most important assignments Dr. Sinclair took on in 1996 was helping Brian conquer his well-founded fears of Kitzbühel, as they jointly developed a strategy for the skier to take himself successfully down the hill again. The paradox was how Dr. Sinclair, on the one hand, worked psychologically with Brian but, on the other, bluntly expressed her own real-world description of Kitzbühel.

"It's an ice rink, and to me, it's a scary place," she said. She joked about how she sampled the starting gate when she and other officials from the World Cup team went to "slip the course," which is the act of testing it and getting it smooth and race-ready for the skiers. "I remember putting my tips out over the start, and then I took a look and just backed right out of the start. I went past the racers and the coaches and said, 'Nope.'"

With Brian, Dr. Sinclair explained, one key was to move his mind away from his emotions and his fear. "We had to get off how he felt and get rid of the distracters and derailers along the way," she said, especially in the section where Brian had crashed. "I had to find tangible things he could do and say to himself to stay in the moment. What are your cues? What do you stay focused on?" Additionally, Dr. Sinclair worked to reinforce how critical it was for Brian to be forward in his stance versus staying back and playing it safe—no easy task with a mountain as formidable as Kitzbühel.

As grateful as Dr. Sinclair was to have Brian recognize her for how much she'd helped him, she was emphatic about who deserved credit. "He did it, not me," she said. "I did my bit, but he's the guy. He did all this. He figured out what he needed to do." She said Brian's mental makeup was a major strength. "Psychologically, he's different from others. Top performers generally do several things really well. He's a patient, methodical, thoughtful person. He can analyze. He can get calm and stay there. And that's a difference maker for me."

With both his mind and his body in a better place, Brian began to see Nagano 1998 as his time, his place. "He was so dialed in," Karen said. "He trained like crazy, and he had this relaxed aggression."

Lalande said the whole Canadian team, weary of "always chasing the Europeans," felt confident about Nagano. They had a course they liked, their own place in the Olympic Village, their own chef, and a short trip to the ski hill for training runs. "There was no stress," he said. The outlook seemed even brighter, Lalande shared, when Canada's skiers performed well during all three training runs leading up to the final. Brian's teammates for those Nagano Olympics included Kevin Wert, Ed Podivinsky—who won a bronze medal at the 1994 Games in Lillehammer—and Luke Sauder, who finished twenty-seventh in the downhill in Lillehammer.

The happy-go-lucky outlook for Canada and all the other skiers took a hit when a one-meter-thick blanket of snow dumped on Nagano. The onslaught of snow combined with extreme winds led a committee of race officials to twice postpone the final. Lalande said Canada's team was never able to train from the top of the ski hill after that.

When race day did come, Lalande said, it was still very windy, creating a more perilous course for the competitors. Skiing publications will tell you that heavy winds are a hazard for downhill skiers because their races are so dependent on ski-tip control and stability. One casualty of the stiff Nagano winds was the great Hermann Maier of Austria. Maier captured gold medals in the super G and giant slalom events later in the Winter Games, but on this downhill course, he was one of those who suffered a spectacular fall and did not finish.

One other setback for Brian came with his draw for the start. Competitors who draw the lower numbers, such as one through fifteen, get to race first in fresher, softer, and more powdery snow, while those drawing higher numbers often face a harder, icier course. The top-ranked skiers drew for numbers one through fifteen in this competition, while Brian and other skiers who weren't ranked as high were in a random draw starting with number sixteen. Brian initially drew number thirty—twice—which would have resulted in him starting his run long after the top skiers—and in the hardest and iciest conditions. But the random draws were redone after the race cancellations, and Brian ended up with number twenty.

No matter the race number, Brian's confidence remained in high gear. "It didn't matter—I knew I was going to win," he said. "It was like I had that gold medal in one pocket and my race number in the other."

Only three weeks after suffering a torn ACL, Brian Stemmle competes in his first of four Winter Olympic Games, in Calgary in 1988. Credit: © Malcolm Carmichael

Breaking from the start and through the early gates of the 2.04-mile-long course, Brian's visualizations seemed prescient. He was leading the downhill. His sister was watching from home and yelled after the first interval, "He's winning!"

The intervals, or segments of the course, are typically about twenty seconds apart, with the first and second intervals equating to about a third and two-thirds of the way down the race hill, respectively. Brian indeed led the downhill race after the first interval, and that was the case after the next interval as well. By his estimation, he was at least 75 percent of the way down the hill when his luck turned. Karen and Dr. Sinclair were pretty sure he was even closer to the finish than that, with only a single turn and two jumps remaining.

"Can you imagine the story?" Lalande asked. "He was right there. What a movie *that* would have made."

But there would be no Hollywood ending for Brian. Recalling that last turn, when he stuck his left ski in the ground and lost his right edge, he said, "It just caught me." He almost high-sided, referring to a moment when the skis lose their grip and slide out of control. "I thought I was going to fall." He was able to keep his balance, but he had missed a gate in the process, and in the blink of an eye, he went from being a potential gold-medal winner to a DNF—"Did Not Finish." Brian, of course, did not medal, nor did his Canadian teammates.

The suddenness of it all jarred not only Brian but also those around him, including his competition. "For a long time, I think he ran it over and over in his head," Karen said, vividly remembering the respect shown by Jean-Luc Crétier of France, the eventual gold winner, who held off celebrating until Brian had made his own run down the mountain. Even years later, at the 2018 Winter Games in Pyeongchang, Brian was with the CBC team providing television coverage when Hannes Trinkl, who had won a bronze medal for Austria at that Winter Olympics in Nagano, came up to Brian. "To this day, I would take fourth place," he said. "You should have won a medal. It was your time."

If anyone could relate to how hard Brian worked, how fanatically he trained, how many times he had visualized that run and that day ending differently, it was Dr. Sinclair. "It was the only time at a sporting event that I cried," she said. "I was at the finish, and I thought I had it together . . . When I saw Brian, neither of us could say anything, and we couldn't help but just cry. [Brian] tried with all his might to finish that last turn, tried as hard as he could to hold out—and he almost did it. You have to be emotionally brave to do that."

Lalande described the night as a "really, really sad evening" and said he lingered over the near miss. "I thought about it for ten years, every day." Even decades later, Lalande wondered about Brian. He was such an elegant skier that it seemed, at least to those on the outside, that everything came easily to him. Could that have worked against him in some way?

"Brian always had the tag on his back that he was lazy," Lalande said, "and he was not." But, he continued, "maybe he was missing a bit of the killer mentality." Lalande said there were other less talented members of the Canadian team with over-the-top work ethics. Could sustained tenacity or more training have made the difference? "We'll never know," he said.

Dr. Sinclair pushed back on that notion. She said there are common misconceptions about the "just try harder, work harder, train harder" line of thinking. "There's a lot of talk in sports about work ethic, but there's more to it than that," she said. "Talent gets you there, but it is the mindset that keeps you there. [Brian] had a calmer composure, and he could keep his reactions in check. That's misinterpreted. People think, *Oh, he doesn't want it enough.* Brian's urgency looks different than others, and people don't get it. Everybody at that level works hard. He had a quiet urgency and a quiet confidence that people should try to emulate more."

Brian would combine his DNF in the downhill with a twelfth-place finish in the super G event. The 1998 Winter Games were the last of his four Olympic appearances. But the Olympics were only part of an impressive résumé that included being on three World Championship teams, participating on the national team from 1985 to 1999, competing in fifteen seasons of World Cup skiing, attaining seven podium finishes, and capturing medals in five Canadian championships. Closer to home, Brian's hometown lauded both him and Karen by inducting them into the Aurora Sports Hall of Fame, and his long journey as a skier also spawned offers to be a CBC Winter Games broadcaster and a motivational speaker.

Heck, he even kept up his side gig of sparring with the foreboding Kitzbühel, skiing it several more times and falling twice more, winding up with a separated shoulder in January 1999 during a training run. He said the year he returned to the mountain, the Norwegian skier behind him "picked up his skis, left the start shack, took the gondola back down, and retired."

Looking back, Brian still lamented the medal finish that wasn't. "I kind of pooched that one away," he said, even with a clear-eyed perspective about the rich and "awesome" career he'd had. He remembered with fondness that first Olympics in Calgary, especially the opening ceremonies where "we walked in, and everyone was cheering." He remembered and appreciated the practices, the training, the slog of staying with competitive skiing for a decade and a half.

"I guess when you look back, it's the hard work, the sacrifices you make, the sacrifices everyone makes," he said. He was philosophical about all of it and came to terms with the fact that his career was a rewarding one, even if it didn't result in shiny medals from a Winter Games. "I didn't quite seize that moment of destiny, but I'm OK with it," Brian said. "It all seems to have flown by . . . too quickly." The

Kitzbühel tragedy and all the injuries were not the only life challenges he faced. Brian and his sister lost both parents prematurely—Andrea to a brain tumor in 2010 and Wilf to complications from a torn aorta in 2014.

He said, "I tell the kids, 'Make sure you cherish every moment.'" The kids he referred to are the twin girls he and his wife, Heather, have together. Brooke and Taylor both grew up to become good athletes and skiers, but without plans to head down the trails that Karen and Brian plowed.

That was OK with Brian, who, along with his broadcasting and motivational-speaking duties, tried to log a lot of hours as a stay-at-home dad for the twins. He said he'd be on board with whatever professional and recreational endeavors his girls might choose. "I would support them in anything they do."

While Brian allowed that a part of him would have loved to see them view the world from ski hills as he did, a bigger part of his DNA was relieved they won't. "I saw what my parents went through—the torment they went through again and again. I just feel like I'd be reliving what I went through," which included a near-death experience on a mountain, a ski career of highs (mostly) and lows, and a quartet of Olympic Games in four countries. But his human touch, not his skiing flair, was the thing that tugged at the emotional nerves of those close to him.

Karen loved what a good father Brian became and saw the magnetic appeal he had. "If you ask him today, I think he'd say his best accomplishment is being an awesome dad." She said there isn't anybody that doesn't want a piece of Brian, from Heather to the kids to a large cast of friends. "Everyone loves my brother. He's just a fun guy to be around."

Dr. Sinclair will always consider him a lifelong friend. Recently, they had a chance to connect. And how did that go? "We cried," she said, with a laugh.

Lalande said he and Brian transitioned from a coach–skier relationship to good friends near the end of Brian's career, transitioning to golfing regularly and remaining close companions. In fact, a keepsake from Brian remains one of Lalande's prized possessions: a framed starting bib from a race in Garmisch-Partenkirchen with a message on the back that neatly encapsulated both a friendship and a skier's summary of his career:

Benny,

Thank you for always steering me in the right direction. Not only on the slopes but more importantly off the slopes. You always knew how to motivate me and guide me in the proper way. I greatly appreciate all the time and effort you spent into making some of my dreams come true.

CHAPTER 7

TOM HINTNAUS, USA

POLE VAULT, 1980 SUMMER OLYMPICS, MOSCOW (US BOYCOTTED)

Spend time around those closest to Tom Hintnaus, and you will quickly learn about the former world-class pole vaulter's competitive juices—a maniacal will to win that transcended traditional sports. Tom's capacity to convert *anything* into a competition is the stuff of family-and-friends lore, with Tom turning every activity into a survival-of-the-fittest contest for the ages.

It is perhaps the cruelest of ironies, then, that one of the most intense competitors on the planet ran into an impenetrable wall that precluded him from testing himself against other elite athletes across the globe. The stop sign that stifled him in 1980 came not from his sport, his opponents, his health and fitness, or his athletic shortcomings, but from his own country.

What happened to Tom that year was the equivalent of a political audible—a last-second change that defies the usual playbook. Athletes, you see, are used to rehabbing from injuries and setbacks. They know precisely how to train to win or to excel. They are hardwired to plan for games and meets, events and competitions. These qualities are woven into the ethos that makes them who they are.

But how do those same athletes deal with a psychological setback they cannot anticipate or prepare for? What happens when the injury is not to the body but to the psyche? What happens when they get themselves pumped up for a game or a contest, only to have their nation let the air out of the figurative tires?

These are the questions, all packaged into a savage mental blow, that confronted Tom. The kid who grew up in Southern California and attended the University of Oregon, the kid who won the 1980 Olympic Trials. He was at the apex of what would have been a celebrated pole-vaulting career. The possibilities for Olympic glory and a shiny medal seemed limitless.

But the Summer Games that year were in Moscow—the cultural, spiritual, athletic, and economic center of a country that had enraged nations throughout the world with its brazen invasion of Afghanistan. In the same way that the international community flashed anger and ire over Russia's unprovoked attack of Ukraine in 2022, many world leaders circa 1979–80 decried the Soviet entry into Afghanistan as an inexcusable violation of human rights, the rule of law, and the principles of peace.

With the United States as a ringleader, and following a series of negotiations that failed to achieve any compromise, some sixty-seven nations ultimately boycotted the 1980 Summer Games in Moscow. One publication from that era said the boycotting nations wanted to hurt the USSR where the Soviets would feel it the most—in their ego. Unfortunately, the smack to that ego ended up inflicting significant pain on hundreds of US athletes harboring hopes of competing in the 1980 Summer Games.

"We heard rumors the president was going to boycott when we were at the [Olympic] Trials," recalled Tom, who loved his adopted country but did not see anything tangible come of the boycott. "It didn't do anything . . . All it did was ruin our lives. They used us as pawns." That was the mindset for many talented, disillusioned athletes like Tom, who were bullish on the United States yet also saw that all they had worked for was thrown asunder in a New York minute. "That was my biggest shot [at a medal] in my life," he said.

After winning the 1980 Olympic Trials, Tom Hintnaus sets the bar at a world record height of 18'11¼". Here he is, taking a shot at it. Credit: Tom Hintnaus

Tom would recover from that psychological takedown to return to the Olympics in 1984, albeit with a twist. He would by happenstance enjoy a lucrative modeling career that had modest origins going back to 1979. He would find success in several business ventures during and after his athletic career. He would marry twice and father two cherished daughters, who took their own roundabout paths to the pole vault. His pathway through life would be productive and robust.

But to comprehend how Tom worked up to the point of being an Olympic athlete, to understand the significance of the mental wallop he absorbed, and to learn about where his competitive spirit took root, it's important to harken back to South America, where Tomás Valdemar Hintnaus was born.

The children of Czechoslovakian parents who hoped to make their way to America, Tom and his older sister, Dagmar, were born in Brazil—she in 1953, he in 1958. After a stop in Germany, his Czech-speaking father and mother, Lubomir and Marianne, had applied to come to the United States. At that time, they were subject to a quota system that had been in place dating back to 1924 that favored immigrants from northern and western European nations. It also limited total immigration visas to 2 percent of the total number of people of each nationality living in the United States at the time of the 1890 census.

Although Congress ended the quota system with a new Immigration and Nationality Act in 1965, that didn't help Lubomir and Marianne. The quota net that was in place and that ensnared Tom's mom and dad—plus a bout of tuberculosis his father contracted—meant an eleven-year wait for them to enter the United States. They spent nine of those years in Brazil, where they conceived their kids.

Tom was two years old when the family relocated to Southern California. They brought with them a love of sports; Lubomir played soccer and Marianne threw the discus well enough to set a state record for her age group. Their kids inherited the sporting gene and played a wide variety of sports day and night.

"[My parents] gave me total freedom," Tom said. "I would play until it would be dark outside." As a kid, he sampled everything from surfing to volleyball, as well as gymnastics, especially since his sister was a talented gymnast. He tagged along with her and learned tumbling, turning movements, and body control, skills that would serve him well in later years. Both his parents were part of the gymnastics Sokol clubs that had originated in Czechoslovakia and had spread all the way to Los Angeles. Tom's dad also served as one of the early coaches for the SCATS (Southern California Acro Team) Gymnastics program, and Dagmar was a teammate of the great Cathy Rigby, who competed on the US gymnastics team in both the 1968 and 1972 Summer Olympics. Dagmar also was an alternate for the 1972 US Olympic team.

Despite all the exposure to gymnastics, it was a different sport that took hold as Tom's number one when he was eight years old. He recalled his dad taking him to the Los Angeles Coliseum, the venue for the 1932 Summer Olympics and the 1984 Games. There, he watched a dual track meet between the United States and the Soviet Union and was transfixed by a pole-vault competition that included Bob Seagren, who went on to win an Olympic gold medal in 1968 and silver in 1972. Fans in the stadium were going crazy, and Tom turned to his dad and said, "That's what I am going to do when I grow up." Lubomir simply patted him on the head.

Undaunted, Tom began maneuvering broomsticks, bamboo poles, and anything else he could get his hands on to vault with. He tried to clear a seven-and-a-half-foot ivy fence in the backyard—and then one day, he did, painfully. "It knocked the wind out of me. I think I lay there for about two minutes." Asked what kind of reaction he got, Tom said his parents "thought it was par for the course for me. I did a lot of wild things as a kid."

The wild thing of pole vaulting stuck with Tom, intensifying after he began his track-and-field career at Aviation High School in Redondo Beach. He was inspired by a track coach named Bill Blewett, who coached at a nearby high school and had been childhood friends with the coach at Tom's school. Blewett first saw Tom playing soccer and was impressed with his talent, and then upon learning that the multisport kid was taking up a new one, he came to watch Tom pole vault.

"He and I just bonded, and I started flourishing," Tom said, adding that Blewett moved over to coach at Aviation High and helped him soar. With Blewett's tutelage and his own commitment to the sport, Tom matured rapidly as a pole vaulter. He jumped personal bests of 12' his freshman year; 14'2¾" as a sophomore; 15'3" as a junior; and 16'5" as a senior. "I ended up being the number-one pole vaulter in the nation," he said, "and I went on to win the California state meet and the United States national meet."

Tom then took a curve to the north with his pole vaulting, transitioning from the sunshine of Southern California to the more inclement weather at the University of Oregon. Although Oregon had a rich and successful track-and-field heritage and the city of Eugene staked out a reputation as TrackTown USA, Tom really hadn't heard of the Ducks' program outside of iconic middle- and long-distance runner Steve Prefontaine. He was more familiar with Oregon's men's basketball program, which had pulled a huge upset win over a UCLA team coached by the legendary John Wooden—just one month after UCLA's nearly three-year-long, eighty-eight-game winning streak had been snapped.

But Tom was swayed after Frank Morris, the field events coach for the Ducks, came to Aviation High to see him compete and take first place in the pole vault, high jump, high hurdles, and low hurdles. Morris, who later went on to serve as a head coach for both Oregon State University and Arizona State University, offered Tom a full-ride scholarship to the University of Oregon.

"I knew that the Olympic Trials were held there [in Eugene] in 1972 and again in 1976," Tom recalled, "and I hoped the 1980 Olympic Trials would be there as well." He arrived at the Oregon campus in 1976 with a goal of winning those Olympic Trials on his home field.

Soon, he got used to vaulting high—very high—for Oregon. Just as sprinter Manteo Mitchell spoke of finding the Hayward Field magic, so, too, would Tom. In his sophomore year, he jumped just over 17'8", taking second at the NCAA Championships to the University of California's Mike Tully, who would go on to set three US pole-vault records and earn a silver medal at the 1984 Summer Games. After a disappointing turn at the NCAAs as a junior, Tom returned as a senior to take second, again, in the NCAA championships.

While winning and losing defines pole vaulters, an interesting sidelight to the event is that it is staged in such a way where athletes often spend a great deal of time together between jumps. As such, competitors often battle intensely during a competition, then segue to being close friends afterward.

That was the case with Tom and Anthony Curran. Curran followed his older brothers into pole vaulting, winning a state championship his senior year of high school and setting what was then a national high school record with a vault of 17'4¼". He attended UCLA, one of Oregon's track-and-field archrivals, and finished fourth in the NCAAs in 1979, second in 1981, and fourth again in 1982. He and Tom attempted to beat each other's brains out in competition but became close friends away from it.

"We hit it off like brothers," said Curran, who was two grades below Tom. "There was a rivalry there, but we were always super friendly with one another. We couldn't wait to get to meets and goof off together." The two former vaulters have had a long run of goofing off together ever since, finding ways to take on a myriad of adrenaline-junkie sports together, from surfing to skiing to hang gliding. "Pole vaulters are thrill seekers," Curran said. The two competitors eventually also became neighbors, maintaining homes on the Hawaiian island of Oahu that were only about fifty yards from one another.

The years the two men spent training together, combined with an illustrious thirty-seven years of coaching pole vaulters at UCLA, gave Curran a bird's-eye view into what made Tom great at his craft. "A lot of people aren't committed to getting completely vertical," Curran said, and "a lot of guys couldn't get as vertical as Tom."

Another skill that helped Tom, who by his own admission lacked the speed of most other jumpers, involved his ability to maneuver and torque his body into prime position for a vault. "I probably wasn't the best-suited for the sport," Tom said, contrasting his own speed with that of the legendary Sergey Bubka, the 1988 gold-medal-winning Ukrainian jumper who broke the world record an astonishing thirty-five times during his career.

"Bubka could run one meter faster a second than me," Tom continued, so he compensated with the skills he learned back in those SCATS gymnastics days. "I did a gymnastics move on the middle of the pole—I just had a knack and a feel for how to do it." Curran added that, for Tom, "it was being aware of his body and how to harness energy."

Another pole vaulter who got an up-close-and-personal sense of what made Tom tick was Jon Switzer, a fellow Southern Californian who followed Tom to the University of Oregon, earning All-America honors in 1980 as he finished tied for fifth in the NCAA championships and paired that with a seventh-place finish at the 1980 Olympic Trials. He agreed that gymnastics skills helped Tom with both maneuverability and strength but said there was another area where his Oregon teammate raised the bar. "He had the best plant I had ever seen at that time," Switzer said, adding that "the plant was everything in pole vaulting, because it got you in position to go [straight] up."

Together with his physical abilities, Tom brought to the pole-vault runway a mental toughness and want-to that made him better. "He's a nonstop competitor," Curran said, "and that made him great."

Ah, yes—that competitive streak. If competitiveness is a burning fire for some, consider it a raging inferno for Tom. Those in his family and inner circle can scarcely go more than a few minutes without talking about it, albeit with a tone of endearment and a playful shake of their heads.

Tom's first daughter, Sage, said, "Everything we did was a competition. We never left a competition unless somebody was crying or bleeding, and we always came back for more." The competition extended to all activities, even "who could cut the smallest slice of cheese," she went on, with a laugh. Tom's youngest daughter, Tommi, said, "If there's a game, he's always playing. Nothing holds him down." Tommi is known for being virtually as competitive as her dad, or even more so, according to him, and the two feverish competitors are typically placed on opposite teams of the family games of "SUP Polo"— essentially water polo on stand-up paddleboards. But Tommi loves the nonstop battles, which also extend to surfing and who can catch the biggest wave. In those contests, her dad can get a bit ruthless. "He won't stop even if he's running you over. We have pictures of people being run over by his board." Tom clarified, "It's all in good fun . . . It gets crazy, but nobody ever gets hurt."

Switzer recalled mixing it up with Tom at practice in a game called moonball, where the vaulters would spend hours a day jumping on a trampoline and throwing a ball through a hoop. "We were always fighting it out," he said, calling Tom "competitive to the last breath." But "it was competitive where we would help each other. There was a camaraderie that's built over time and makes you part of a small clique . . . It's a fraternity where you help each other reach higher heights."

Curran, who traveled much of the world to national and international track meets with Tom, said contests of all kinds were a day-and-night vocation. "We were throwing paper airplanes out the hotel window on the fifteenth floor to see who could fly them the furthest . . . We would race from the bus to the doorway of the hotel." Added Paul Viggiano, a pastor and former track-and-field athlete who lived with Tom two different times in the early to mid-1980s: "We would play video games, and if he didn't win, he wouldn't let me go to bed. We would stay up until three or four in the morning. I would lose out of sheer attrition."

With that backdrop, take Tom's tenacious competitiveness and zero in on 1980. Blend in four years of stellar vaulting—all while taking on some of the best vaulters in the world in the then Pac-10

Conference and at the NCAA championships. It was a recipe for being ready, being great, and feeling like it's your time. Tom certainly did, and the Olympics were his dream. "I was more than ready to go. It was like tunnel vision. I focused on competing, and I really didn't party like many of the other students did." In a three-week period of June 1980, he ended up second in the NCAAs, won the US National Championships, and won the Olympic Trials.

Tom had reason, beyond those results, to feel confident about his chances internationally. When he won the Olympic Trials, he'd had the pole-vault bar placed at a world record 18'11¼" high. "I had three really good attempts at the world record at the Trials," he said, "and, actually, on one of them, it was just the wind that blew the bar back over . . . I was jumping the best I ever had." Added Switzer of those world-record attempts: "He was right there."

It was achingly disappointing, then, that the guy who was "right there" couldn't be there for Moscow. Instead, Tom represented the United States and won at a Liberty Bell Classic track-and-field event in July 1980 that was dubbed the "Olympic Boycott Games." Tom faced six other pole vaulters in the event—about a third the size of the field he would have faced off against in Moscow.

But more than that, even though the Liberty Bell Classic attracted three hundred athletes from twenty-six nations, it was widely viewed as a poor consolation prize, at best, for Tom and many other competitors. Later that year, as one of several hundred recipients of a Congressional Gold Medal created for the athletes who were subjected to the boycott, Tom gritted his teeth and went to the White House for a ceremony. It was all political window dressing, and it leaves one wondering what Tom could have done—would have done—had he trekked to Moscow in the Summer of 1980. "Back then, 95 percent of the time, the guy who wins the US Olympic Trials wins the gold," he said.

Of the pole vaulters who did attend the Moscow Games, six of them broke the Olympic record of 5.5 meters, which equates to 18' ½". Poland's Wladyslaw Kozakiewicz won the event with a world-record vault of 5.78 meters, or just over 18'11½". He had cleared a height a mere quarter inch higher than the one Tom had attempted and just missed clearing one month earlier. So how would Tom have stacked up?

That is of course a game of supposition, but Tom's college teammate

Switzer and his friendly rival Curran have every reason to believe their friend would have medaled—if not more. "I'd say top three, bar none. He would have risen to the occasion," Switzer said. "You know, he could have won the thing if he was hot that day. It comes down to how hot you were at the time."

Curran said, "Since he was so dialed in, I think he would have medaled." He added that it is a foreboding sight to see pole-vault bars positioned 19' and 20' up in the air. "I don't know how I did that . . . and most people would not put themselves through that pain. To get a medal is out of control."

Of course, what was most out of control for Tom was any ability to reverse an international boycott. It wasn't to be, and so he would be put through a major competition of another sort: a test of the mind, soul, and mental psyche. Confidants said the boycott spotlighted another characteristic that is a hallmark of Tom's resiliency. Moping and self-pity do not occupy much space within his DNA.

"A lot of us were very put off. It all became something the Olympics aren't supposed to be," Viggiano said. "Even if the world is crumbling, the Olympics is supposed to be a place where international competitors can shake hands and fight it out."

In my humble opinion, Viggiano accurately put his finger on the ideal the International Olympic Committee *strives for* in staging the Olympics. Yet a review of the actions the United States and other nations have taken when a cloud of war and turbulence has hung over the Olympics shows a mixed record. World Wars I and II both led to the cancellations of Olympic Games. Yet in 1936, years after Hitler had already begun his ruthless grab for world power, celebrated US athletes like Jesse Owens famously used the Summer Games in Berlin to erase the Third Reich's myth that Aryan athletes somehow possessed athletics skills that were superior to others. Post–World War II, neither the Korean War nor the Vietnam War kept the Olympic Games from marching on. More recently, Russia's invasion of Ukraine failed to trigger any Western nations boycotting, or attempting to halt, the 2024 Summer Games in Paris.

Regardless of whether America's 1980 Olympics boycott could be justified on any level, Viggiano said Tom showed a remarkable ability to move on. "Tom is the kind of guy [where] his spirit is not going to be quelled. There wasn't this sense of 'poor me, poor me.' We all knew he was not going to be defined by someone else's decision."

Curran said, "If anybody is going to get over things and move on to the next thing, it's Tom. I'm sure he had a broken heart . . . You spend all your time and energy for so many years to reach that goal and accomplish that dream; it's probably the most devastating thing for an athlete. But I don't think he skipped a beat. As devastating as it was, he was healthy and strong, and he had his family and friends supporting him."

All that was true, but while Tom turned the page, forgetting was a tougher challenge. He would move on, but he couldn't shake the feeling of being abandoned by a country that fired a political shot that left him and other athletes unfairly wounded. Tom knew that, as an athlete born in Brazil, he had an opportunity to compete for the South American nation in 1984.

He talked to Brazil's governing body in 1981–82 "to see if it was possible," he said. "They invited me to come down and compete in some of their meets, and I ended up getting on the team for the [1983] World Championships in Helsinki." Tom acknowledged, too, that it was also easier for him to make Brazil's national team vis-à-vis taking on a bevy of elite vaulters vying for the US team.

He ended up finishing fifth in the World Championships, placing ahead of all three Americans in the field. He also won a bronze medal at the 1983 Pan American Games competing for Brazil. He was on track to go to the Los Angeles Olympics in 1984, where he would, ironically, represent a South American country despite having grown up a short bus ride from the Olympic Coliseum where the track-and-field events would be staged.

A quirk of Tom's time competing for Brazil was that he fared well leading up to the 1984 Summer Games, and he jumped successfully afterward, landing an 18' 10¾" vault at a meet in Zurich, which stood as a Brazilian national record until 2007. Unfortunately, *during* the 1984 Summer Games, fate would not be as kind to Tom. Ironically, he was one of two University of Oregon athletes who competed for Brazil in the 1984 Games. The other, Joaquim Cruz, won gold in the 800 meters. But in the pole vault, Tom would not get near that rarefied air. He had one high jump where he came down on the pole-vault cross bar,

Tom Hintnaus soars to victory at the 1980 Olympic Trials with vaults like this one.
Credit: Tom Hintnaus

but otherwise he struggled with swirling wind in the LA Coliseum. He also dealt with bursitis leading up to the Games and broke his prized pole in warmups before the finals. Although he made the finals, he placed twelfth. His 1984 Olympics experience would be a bittersweet one. "I hate excuses," he said. "Sometimes, it doesn't go your way."

That 1984 pole-vault competition went the way of Frenchman Pierre Quinon, who took gold. Americans Mike Tully and Earl Bell captured silver and bronze—with Bell sharing third place with Thierry Vigneron of France. The stars had been aligned for Tom in 1980, but they were crisscrossed in 1984. Curran said that unfortunately can be the nature of the sport, which has more variables than virtually any other track-and-field event. As one who coached both men and women jumpers and tutored multiple Olympians, national record holders, and NCAA and Pac-12 Champions during his tenure at UCLA, he has seen it all.

"One time you hit a home run, the next time you might strike out," he said. "There are so many obstacles in the way. Your step has to be right; the standards have to be in the right place. You might deal with changing poles; maybe the winds are crossing. All these things can get in your way as you're trying to fix one . . . People don't understand how difficult it is to be a consistent top-level vaulter."

The thing is, while August 8, 1984, went south on him, pole vaulting remained Tom's guiding North Star for several more years. He continued to jump internationally, finally putting his poles away after going to South Africa and competing in 1988–89. He then went on to play on a pro beach volleyball tour from 1991 to 1994 to satiate that competitive spirit. "That was *really* fun," Tom said, "like I went to Fantasy Island and had a whole other career."

Actually, along with pro volleyball, Tom had *other* careers, including one that initially began in 1979 and exploded after a chance meeting with a fashion-design icon. That career—one that helped finance over a decade worth of pole vaulting and volleyball—was, well, underwear. Calvin Klein underwear to be exact.

There is a tall tale that Klein himself initially spun for the media, with the fashion mogul saying he saw muscular Tom running along Sunset Boulevard in 1982 and uttered to his driver, "That's him. Stop the car!" Well, not quite. In truth, Tom said he had been modeling for three years when he first got hired to model Calvin Klein underwear in 1982. Soon after, Klein mentioned they were heading to Greece to introduce a big new product line, and Tom was to meet them there, without telling anyone.

While Klein had conjured up a somewhat fictionalized account of how he had cast Tom in the role of underwear model, what happened next was the real deal. When renowned photographer Bruce Weber took a shot of Tom—tanned, shirtless, and wearing tighty-whitie Calvin Kleins, Tom became the model for the very first major Calvin Klein men's underwear ads. The advertising photo from Greece was soon plastered on a billboard in New York's Times Square and in many other places, and Tom became a famous body for selling male underwear and male sex appeal. His then revolutionary ad was named by *American Photographer* magazine in 1989 as one of "10 Pictures That Changed America."

The ex–pole vaulter's Calvin Klein ads were treated with wry humor, just like many other topics discussed among the Hintnaus family. "That's the irony of the thing," Tom said with a laugh. "I worked really hard to be the best at my sport, and that ad is the thing that is still following me around."

Sage said that when she was little, her mom—Tom's first wife, Michelle—gave her a picture of the Calvin Klein ad, and it got all kinds of laughs when her stepdad said to her mom, "You know she has a poster of a guy in his underwear?"

Tommi said, "It was so weird . . . Your dad in his underwear—really?" She said the Calvin Klein wise cracks followed her during her own pole-vaulting career at ASU, where her coach, Ron Barela, had known Tom from his vaulting days. Barela would tell her what a good vaulter her dad had been, and he'd kiddingly refer to the ads, too. "Ron would always say, 'Your dad was the best-looking guy—looked like a model running down the track.' It was always so embarrassing . . . I would be saying, 'I get it, I get it, Coach B. He was good, and he looked good.'"

Being a Calvin Klein underwear model paid lots of bills for Tom, who took on plenty of other endeavors that worked out well over the years. In his adopted home state of Hawaii, Tom owned and operated Aqua Docks Hawaii Kai, a construction company specializing in residential floating docks and remodeling. He also owned and managed four Airbnbs in Waikiki. Even well into his sixties, Tom still hadn't slowed down much. When I interviewed him, he had just competed in a sixty-and-over softball tournament and remained an avid participant in several outdoor sports.

Tom also experienced the joy of coaching other pole-vault athletes over the years, including two daughters who didn't initially plan to jump but ultimately gravitated to the sport their dad had excelled in. Tommi pole vaulted for both ASU and Kansas State University, reaching a height of 13'11¾" at the conference championships and finishing twelfth in the NCAA championships in 2022. Her achievement was particularly special because those championships were held at the very track where her dad's pole-vaulting career took major flight—Hayward Field. Sage set a school pole-vaulting record for Katy High School near Houston and then vaulted for three years at the University of Houston. She actually set her personal best of 12'10" at a USATF Masters meet after her daughter was born.

Sage and Tommi agreed that life around Tom is never, ever boring.

"My dad told me the worst thing in the world is to be ordinary, and he is anything but ordinary," Sage said. Tommi said she is so proud of him, but playfully cautioned, "Don't tell him that." She called both her mom and dad her number-one motivators and said her dad was in the stands every time she set a personal record.

For Tom, the bitterness in the wake of 1980 long ago gave way to gratitude. He slayed the psychological dragon of the 1980 boycott and propelled himself to a life many would envy. After a seven-year marriage to his first wife, he and his second wife, Jennifer, have been together for more than a quarter of a century. The couple settled on the east side of the island of Oahu, two miles from Hawaii's population center of Waikiki.

"You have that one shot in life—that one bullet. In my case, it just missed," Tom said. But he added, "Other than a couple of setbacks, I've had a storybook life. It's been like a fairy tale."

While Tom described a fairy-tale life, there's one other real-world skill of his that hangs alongside the voracious, competitive fire and the endless resiliency. Turns out that the guy who sprung himself airborne for a living also possessed an uncanny ability to propel others, to make them feel better about themselves, and to pick them up when they were down. His daughters applauded their dad for this quality, but there was also a close friend who credited him with this gift.

Cliff Meidl, who is eight years younger than Tom, called him "a huge, huge part of my life." Both hailed from the same neighborhood in Manhattan Beach, where Meidl delivered newspapers to the Hintnaus house as a kid. He first met Tom when he was a high school sophomore in the spring of 1982, asking whether, despite his frenetic schedule, Tom might consider going down to Aviation High School to volunteer coach the pole vaulters. "Absolutely" came the reply.

While Meidl spoke of Tom's pole-vault coaching creds, that wasn't the thing he held dearest about his friend. That came years later, when Meidl was twenty years old and working a construction job where he had to operate a jackhammer. One day, he jackhammered into an electrical line, and the current to his body nearly cost him his life, temporarily rendering him unable to use his legs. Meidl said he ran into Tom at the local gym when he was on crutches. "I was in dire straits. I was extremely ashamed and felt like I had a lot taken away from me." The road back was a tough one for Meidl, who credited a handful of people with his recovery: the doctors who performed his surgery; his younger brother, Norman, who encouraged him to look for athletic activities he *could* do; and Tom, who offered nonstop positive mentoring, motivation, and encouragement.

Meidl found the sport of sprint kayaking and competed in kayaking events at two Olympic Games. He also developed a successful career in asset management and motivational speaking. In our interview, he emphasized that it wasn't Tom's ability to pole vault toward the sky that made him so great but rather his human touch and how he figured out what was important on the ground. Tom's road to quiet heroism began with the mentally painful challenge of how to rebound from a disappointment foisted on him by a nation's political decision to boycott, a decision that crushed his Olympics dreams. Yet Tom found a path to pursuing other dreams, to raising a family, to motivating others. Meidl aggressively challenged the assertion that Tom never won an Olympic medal.

"He's won the gold medal in life," Meidl said. "He touched me in a way that made a massive difference in my life and provided inspiration to a kid when he really needed it . . . Maybe Tom didn't win a physical gold medal on his wall, but he won a gold medal in inspiring me. He planted a huge hope in my life."

PART III

SPORTSMANSHIP WON

.

CHAPTER 8

TRACY BARNES, USA

WOMEN'S BIATHLON, 2014 WINTER OLYMPICS, SOCHI

For many years, Tracy and Lanny Barnes figured a soccer ball would kick-start their path to the Olympic Games.

The identical twin sisters were born a few minutes apart on April 26, 1982. They grew up sport shooting bows and guns with their dad in the small southwest Colorado town of Durango, some five-and-a-half hours from Denver. They also enjoyed exploring Colorado's majestic trails and mountains with their parents, but they idolized US Women's National Soccer Team (USWNT) stars such as Mia Hamm. Lanny said soccer was clearly their first love. "We really excelled early on. Soccer came easier to us than biathlon."

The sport dubbed "the Beautiful Game" allowed the twins to showcase their athletic ability and their knack for being both physically and mentally strong. They also exhibited a zen-like ability to know exactly what the other was thinking and doing on and off the field, which their father, Thad Barnes, dubbed their "mental telepathy." The sixth sense extended to their verbal back-and-forth as well. "There was a lot of 'we' in their conversation," Thad said. "It always amazed me that they never ran out of things to talk about. They were *so* close."

The sisters took that close relationship outside as often as not, and Lanny recalled how grateful they were to have grown up in an outdoor haven with over three hundred days of sunshine a year. But whether they were outdoors or indoors, the two thrived on desire and one-upping each other. Thad said he and his wife, Deb, kept a Ping-Pong table in the house, but the sport of choice didn't need to be an organized one. "Heck, they could compete at throwing rocks."

To feed that competitive streak, Thad and Deb gave their daughters free rein to try a full range of activities. Tracy and Lanny's older sister, Christie, did some shooting at a local level and tried Nordic skiing. The twins tried all that, plus soccer and basketball and more. Early on, they formed a passion for shooting and delighted in hitting all their targets. Still, the stationary nature of the sport left the action-addicted duo wanting more.

Perhaps that's why the twins' shoot-for-the-stars dream continued with a focus on the soccer pitch. The two forwards watched the USWNT march to Olympic gold in 1996 and kept a close eye on their second of multiple World Cup wins in 1999. As far as they were concerned, they were going to make that team.

The sisters would indeed compete in the Olympic Games, leaving an admirable legacy in their wake. But the headlines they made in the twenty-first century were far different from any they could have foreseen in those closing years of the twentieth.

In the mid-1990s, Tracy and Lanny first became intrigued by the idea of adding the biathlon to their athletic repertoire. A coach named Tim Conrad saw their skills at a small-bore shooting event in middle school and suggested they try biathlon. That led to research and exploration into a sport that is a huge draw in European countries such as Norway but is almost invisible to many US athletes. "It took us a few years to find competitions and learn more about how to get into the sport," said Tracy. Once they did, "we thought it would be a great way to stay in shape for soccer."

Their Olympic goals started to bend a different direction in their senior year of high school, when their small-town school soccer team matched up against teams from the Denver metropolitan area and failed to advance. "Tracy and I were just sitting on the field, and we were crying," said Lanny. "We thought it was just time for us to go over to biathlon." The twins talked more about it, and one night, they made an announcement to their parents that stuck with their dad.

"The US is already on the books for soccer," they told Thad and Deb. The Barnes sisters wanted to carve out a new destination, plowing ground where US women could excel.

"I thought that was a really grown-up way to look at it," Thad said. But biathlon was such a newfound sport, still in its toddler years, in the United States. "We had to look it up."

Biathlon, which combines cross-country skis and poles with rifles, traces its origins to Scandinavian nations where the people once revered a Norse god of hunting and skiing. It was designated an Olympic sport in 1955, and Austria hosted the first Biathlon World Championship in 1958. The 1960 Winter Olympic Games first included biathlon for men, and it was thirty-two more years before women had their first opportunity to compete in the sport on an Olympic stage in France.

Beyond the steep learning curve of any new sport, the Barnes twins had another monumental challenge: they were skiing neophytes. "We were terrible in Nordic skiing," recalled Tracy. "We stuck our heads down and flailed down. You should have seen the looks on the faces of the other girls." Lanny agreed they "were horrible" and recalled that, on her first team outing, she "had no idea" how to get her boots into the bindings. But the challenge of learning something new was attractive to two women athletes who embodied both physical talent and mental toughness. "We were like, we're not quitting until we figure it out," Lanny said.

Cory Salmela, who coached the US Biathlon Junior National Team from 1991 through 2003, agreed that skiing was certainly not the twins' strong suit. They hadn't learned how to carry and manage their oxygen intake like other cross-country skiers who had started years before. His approach to coaching the girls was to mitigate weaknesses and expand their strengths, which included how they brought racing smarts to the table as well as an insatiable work ethic. "You can't train a heart to be bigger," he said, and the twins had maxed out that part of the sport.

Besides, there was a part of biathlon—the shooting—where Tracy

Tracy Barnes competes in the 2013 Biathlon World Championships.
Credit: © US Biathlon / NordicFocus

and Lanny took a back seat to absolutely no one. Their dad said they grew to love the "runnin' and gunnin'" skill set of biathlon. Max Cobb, who was with US Biathlon from 1989 through 2022 and later ascended to serving as the secretary general of the International Biathlon Union (IBU), said, "Obviously they were amazing athletes to start with, and I was amazed at how well they managed the shooting. With their speed and accuracy [in shooting], they were leading performers on the team. These two petite women showing everyone how it could be done—it was super impressive."

Serendipity was also on the side of the twins. According to Salmela, they had joined the Junior National program at precisely the time that US Biathlon decided full-time training and exposure to international events was going to be the only way to get future Olympians from the United States ready to compete against European athletes who stood atop the world. "It was almost like a Junior World Championships every weekend," he said, with US teams regularly traveling abroad to countries like Italy, Austria, Switzerland, and France for three weeks at a time. Along with getting Junior National athletes ready for what they would be facing, the coaches focused on "getting our kids peaking, and we primed the pump with good results."

Cobb added that US Biathlon was "big-time in the shadows into the 1990s. At that time, people would hear 'biathlon' and say, 'Is that swimming and running or biking? What is it?'" But US Biathlon created Regional Centers of Excellence and primarily recruited cross-country skiers to try biathlon. "That was how we were bringing people into the sport," Cobb said, calling it "a thrilling time."

Salmela explained how US Biathlon captured over thirty international medals from 1991 to 2003, and he pointed particularly to 1997, when Jay Hakkinen achieved a Junior World Championship win. Hakkinen finished tenth in the 20-kilometer individual race at the 2006 Winter Games in Turin and led a US relay team that finished in ninth place. Years later, Deedra Irwin recorded a seventh-place finish in the women's 15-kilometer individual event, which was the best Olympic finish ever at that time by a US biathlete.

In 2002, the twins took full advantage of the US Biathlon strategy of training and building up its athletes. They were on a silver-medal-winning 3×7.5-kilometer relay team at the 2002 Junior World Championships in Italy, and Lanny captured a bronze in the 12.5-kilometer individual event. It was a dramatic ascent for the sisters, especially given how every aspect of the sport had been difficult to begin with, and also how Tracy had contracted giardia and threw up at her first international competition.

The twins had some hopes of cracking the US Biathlon Women's Team that year. "We tried out for Salt Lake [City] in 2002, and we did really well," Tracy said. But among other setbacks, they came down with food poisoning. They didn't make the team that year but broke through in 2006, and Tracy described the experience of marching with the US team and hanging out at the Olympic Village as unforgettable. "Our eyes were this big." Added Lanny: "We didn't even have to say anything. To walk into that stadium [for opening ceremonies] and hear everyone chant 'USA, USA!'—I can't even describe it with words."

As Tracy remembered it, the twins didn't miss a target in the shooting competition at those 2006 Games in Turin. But they faltered in the skiing portion. They were both part of a 4×6-kilometer relay team that finished fifteenth out of eighteen teams, and Tracy took fifty-seventh place, and Lanny sixty-fourth, in a 15-kilometer individual event that featured eighty-two competitors.

Throughout their soccer-playing days and well into their biathlon careers, the Barnes twins were inseparable, and they assumed that would always be the case. In 2010, though, the lifelong knot that knitted the two of them came undone.

Leading up to the Olympic Trials for the women's biathlon, where five women competed for four spots on the US team, Tracy shared, "I would've said I would be the one to make the team. A lot of it comes down to confidence. Lanny and I competed together, and the thing that separated us was our confidence." On that front, Tracy felt she was perhaps the steadier competitor, while Lanny was less consistent but prone to pulling out amazing performances.

The 2010 Olympic Trials had a multirace, multilocation format that created an air of unpredictability. "The Trials process is pretty miserable. It's a long, arduous process," Tracy said. It became more arduous for her when, in the first race, she "bombed it." She had a better second race and looked forward to claiming one of the four sports at an IBU cup race that was to cap the Trials competition.

But that morning, with extremely foggy conditions blanketing the course, IBU officials canceled the race, meaning the four women's Olympic spots would be decided based on the prior races. Lanny had survived the gauntlet; her twin sister had not. "I felt I was cheated out of that chance," Tracy said. "I would have liked that one opportunity, and then it would have been decided by the athletes."

Tracy went to the 2010 Winter Olympics in Vancouver, but it was simply to watch her twin sister rather than compete herself. The "ecstasy of victory" versus "agony of defeat" dichotomy came into even sharper focus as 2010 ended up being Lanny's best-ever Olympics performance. She finished twenty-third in the 15-kilometer individual event, which was then one of the best US women's finishes ever, and added a sixteenth-place finish as part of the 4×6-kilometer relay team. "I was very close to getting a medal that day," Lanny recalled. "I think I pulled out motivation that I was not just racing for the USA but also for Tracy." She added that her ski times were right near the top of the pack for four of the first five laps. "I remember thinking, *Hey, we were that close.*"

Meanwhile, for Tracy, 2010 left a stabbing pain that continued to gnaw at her years later. "I was used to the ups and downs of the sport," she said, but she acknowledged it was excruciating to come back from the Trials experience. "Of course, I asked, 'Why me?'" And, in some ways, 2010 was just as difficult for Lanny. The kinetic connection between the two sisters had been severed in a way few others could understand. "When she didn't make the team, I was devastated," Lanny explained. "It was the first night of my life we didn't sleep in the same room together."

Fast-forward to 2014, with Tracy feeling she had a wrong to right and Lanny looking to make her third Olympic biathlon appearance. "Again, we both expected to make the team," Tracy said, adding that she was "at the peak" of her training. The twins had another reason for feeling pressure to make the 2014 team headed to Sochi. This, they decided, would be their final chapter of a journey that had begun nearly twenty years earlier. "We decided that 2014 was going to be our last Olympics," Lanny said. She added that she and Tracy had loved their biathlon career, but it had taken a toll on their bodies and on their families. "We didn't spend a Christmas or a Thanksgiving in the US for close to fifteen years."

There was a positive omen looming ahead for the Barnes sisters as they approached the 2014 Games. The women's biathlon Trials would be in Ridnaun, the very place where the twins tasted major success years before at a Junior World Championships. Unfortunately, another cruel twist of fate lay ahead for the twins. This time, the "ecstasy of victory" feeling belonged to Tracy, while Lanny played the "agony of defeat" role.

Tracy was skiing and shooting out of her mind that week—in the zone that elite athletes enter when their performances rise to an otherworldly level. "I had my last race at those Trials," Tracy said, "and it was the best race of my career to that point. That's one of the things you strive for in biathlon, so I was super excited. I don't know if I'd ever felt that way."

But the way Tracy felt off the ski hills and away from the shooting targets was very different. She was suffering alongside her twin sister, who had come down with a nasty upper-respiratory infection right before the first race of the Trials. "That was one of the most difficult weeks ever," Tracy remembered. "Lanny was hacking and coughing a lot . . . I'm sharing a room with Lanny, and I can hear her at night. I knew how she felt."

Tracy rued the fact that a blanket of fog in 2010, followed by a bout of coughing in 2014—"things that are outside our control"—derailed multiple Olympic hopes. "I was feeling helpless throughout that week," she said. "There's not a whole lot you can do. You watch it slip away [for Lanny]. It's so devastating." Underscoring how closely Tracy and Lanny were tethered to each other, her twin sister had used the same term—devastating—to describe Tracy's weather-induced near-miss four years prior.

But as the 2014 Trials were about to wrap, an idea was fermenting in Tracy's mind. Despite being a few minutes younger than Lanny, she considered herself the more mature of the twins and Lanny the more vulnerable one. Tracy kiddingly referred to her at one point as "Lil' Orphan Lanny." Kidding aside, it was becoming clear to Tracy, who felt a sense of helplessness much of the week, that some sisterly assistance just *had* to be brought to the surface.

Then it occurred to Tracy that there indeed *was* a fix to the dilemma that separated her sister from a spot on the Olympic team. What made her solution possible was that she had secured the fourth—and final—spot on the 2014 women's biathlon team. Lanny, on the other hand, was just outside the mix, having missed three of four races and sitting as the alternate in fifth place.

On January 13, the day after the final sprint race of the biathlon Trials, it was time for Tracy to hatch an idea that, "to be honest, I had been toying with all week." She had finalized her decision the night before the final race. Now she would share it with her twin sister.

A restaurant lay atop a hill above where the twins and their teammates stayed for the Trials. The biathletes, including Tracy and Lanny, often skied to the café, but on this night, given Lanny's condition, the sisters walked. And that's when Tracy put an offer on the table that dramatically changed the makeup of the team bound for Sochi—not to mention the course of their Olympic careers. "We were just walking up this road and having this conversation" when she sprang the idea on Lanny.

Tracy would give up her fourth spot on the team in favor of the first alternate—her twin sister. "I talked her into it. I don't know how I convinced her."

Initially, though, Tracy hadn't convinced her sister of a darned thing. "Absolutely not!" came the reply. "I thought she was crazy," said Lanny. "I remember saying, 'No! This is your opportunity. You earned it.' It went back and forth. My twin sister—she's a little stubborn." But finally it occurred to Lanny that there was no talking her sister out of this decision. "I said, 'All right, Tracy, I will go, and I will race.'"

While the sisters had come to a joint decision, the ultimate call was not theirs to make. The twins were pretty sure it was possible for the last person on a team to decline a spot, and for the first alternate to take it. But Tracy knew that to make it official, she would have to talk to Cobb, who at that point was president of US Biathlon. The conversation came that same night.

"Are you sure?" asked Cobb. It was the most diplomatic phrase he could use to challenge whether an elite athlete who had just demonstrated that this was *her* time should sacrifice a trip to an Olympic Games. "That's why the emotion sticks with me today, because I do recognize the sacrifice every athlete makes," he said. "It was an incredible, unselfish, generous thing to do." Cobb ran the decision through all the formal channels, and then it became official. When the rest of the women's biathlon team received the news, they were shocked. "I don't think anybody really knew what to say," Lanny said.

Salmela, who was in Sochi to help NBC Sports broadcast the biathlon events to their US audience, remembers that it was the NBC *news* team that took the lead on conveying Tracy's story. But while he didn't join in the telling of it, he understood it. "Tracy was always a team player—the mother taking care of other people, even me. It didn't really surprise me."

Whether this was a shocking moment or a more understandable one, it was no rash decision on Tracy's part. She said she was "completely happy and content at this point." She knew she was not going to win a medal, and she honestly felt her sister would have a better chance of doing so. The full statement released by Team USA revealed the selfless thought process Tracy had sorted through before doing what she did:

"And as the old saying goes . . . 'Only the strong will survive.' Most of the time, that is the case. On occasion, the strong don't survive for whatever reason. And that is what I feel happened to Lanny. She's having a stellar season, and she's bound to do great things this year, but she fell ill during the Trials and couldn't race. Because of that, she didn't make the team. While most people would say, 'That's biathlon, or that's life'— and they'd be absolutely correct in saying that—but what if that person who was hit with a little bit of bad luck got a second chance? What if someone believed in them enough to give them that chance? Well, that's what I did. Easy decision.

"Lanny is my best friend and my teammate. I see how hard she works on a daily basis, so I know firsthand that she is deserving of a spot on the Olympic Team. If I can be the one to give her that opportunity, then that is an honor and a sacrifice that I am willing to make."

In an email sent to the Associated Press after her decision went public, Tracy added, *"If you care enough about a person, you will make any sacrifice for them. Even if it means giving up your dreams so that they can realize theirs."*

It would be wonderful for this story to climax with a thrilling, medal-winning, record-setting trip to Sochi for Lanny. That didn't happen. She placed a distant sixty-first in the 15-kilometer event, which she believed was because she hadn't fully recovered from the respiratory infection and tried *too* hard to make Tracy proud of her. "I went out too hard and bombed," she said. Yet she learned an important lesson about finishing and doing her best. "The biggest thing I learned was that I wasn't a quitter," she said. "I didn't win a medal, but I gave every ounce of energy for my sister and my country."

Tracy, too, had put tremendous energy into getting her twin sister to that Winter Games, and there is simply no denying the magnitude of the sacrifice she made that day. But it raises an interesting question: If that teammate in the alternate spot had been someone other than her twin sister, perhaps a close competitor and friend, would Tracy have done the same thing? If it had been "Lanny Smith" rather than Lanny Barnes, would Tracy have given up her spot?

"For me, I've probably experienced a lot more defeat in sports than

Tracy Barnes (right) and Lanny Barnes (left) pose for the cover of Teen People in 2005, just months before their first Winter Games appearance for Team USA. Credit: © US Biathlon / NordicFocus

triumphs," Tracy said. "So, I've developed a sense of appreciation for that and how those athletes are feeling. Had I not been a twin, it might have been different." But as a twin, she said, it's like "you're literally born into a marriage. It's shaped who I am." As a result, she said, "My [real] husband and I rarely fight." And in response to the question of whether she would have given up her spot for a teammate other than her twin, she said she'd "like to say I would do it for someone else. Life is tough sometimes."

Incredibly, when asked the same question—and without knowing how Tracy had responded—her father, her twin sister, her Junior Nationals coach, and the US Biathlon president all arrived at the same answer.

"I'd like to think that she would, because that's who Tracy is," Lanny said.

"If she thinks it's right, it's right," Thad said.

"I think if it's Lanny 'Smith' and she was a strong contender . . . Tracy knew her limits, and she would have done it," Salmela said. "Only she would know," added Cobb, but "I could see her doing it."

It has been over a decade since that January 2014 night when Tracy Barnes went viral for selfless sportsmanship rather than superlative athletic skills. She and her family members and coaches have scattered to different parts of the United States—and the world.

Tracy and her husband, Gary Colliander, a talented athlete and Nordic ski coach for the US team at the 2018 Paralympic Games, remained in Durango, where Tracy runs a property-management company owned by her dad and instructs law-enforcement professionals on the physiological and psychological aspects of shooting and handling stress through her training school, TOP (The Olympian Project) Shooting Institute. Lanny settled with her husband, Grant, near Las Vegas and, as the chief experience officer for PrairieFire Nevada, went on to help design target-shooting sites, ropes courses, mountain trails, and other outdoor experiences. Thad and Deb retired from general-contracting and teaching careers to a house they had built in Alaska in 2007.

With the luxury of a look back on that fateful night, memories of what Tracy did run the gamut, from unassuming to fond to warm to a level akin to the renowned "We're not worthy" bow from *Wayne's World*. Unsurprisingly, the most unassuming view belongs to Tracy, who harbors no regrets and engages in no what-ifs. "Looking back, I was totally content with where I was as an athlete," she said. She had reached what she felt was the high point of her sport, and the lack of a medal didn't change that perspective. "There is more to life than winning [Olympic] medals. Heck, most of my medals from all my races are just sitting in a box, anyway."

The modesty stopped abruptly at the door of her very proud father. "I thought, what a heck of a thing for Tracy to do," said Thad. "It's very selfless that she would do that, and it speaks to the closeness they had. We're still talking about it years later, which is pretty amazing. You know, it's not like she picked up a car to save somebody, but at the same time, it is pretty spectacular."

"It's a very warm memory," said Cobb. "You know, you hope your sports heroes will behave in ways that give you respect more for their conduct off the field than their performance on it. This was one of those times you can say true championship behavior was exhibited."

"Those two had their connection," Salmela said—one that is "really hard for the rest of us to understand. Maybe, in the end, it's the ultimate form of love. Neither of them were going to win medals, so this is about something else other than results."

However, with all due respect to Tracy, her dad, and Salmela and Cobb, perhaps it is fitting that the last words on this subject should come from her twin sister. The level of empathy, caring, sportsmanship, and selflessness demonstrated by Tracy brought out emotions, years later, that were every bit as raw as they were in 2014. Lanny called Tracy "the best and most amazing person on the planet. I put her on a pedestal." The twin sisters talk every day, and Lanny said, "The world isn't quite as good when we're apart. I'm incredibly proud of everything she's done in her life, including that." What Tracy did in January 2014 also left Lanny with a lifelong debt of gratitude. "I'm going to spend the rest of my life trying to repay what she did for me."

CHAPTER 9

LAWRENCE LEMIEUX, CANADA

MEN'S SAILING, FINN CLASS, 1988 SUMMER OLYMPICS, SEOUL

When he was five years old, Lawrence Lemieux yearned to take a sail with his brothers on Wabamun Lake, the nearly twelve-mile-long waterway in Northern Alberta where he and his seven older siblings grew up. On this particular summer day, though, Lawrence's older brother Robert had tired of taking the young tike for rides.

Robert, then thirteen, said to his little brother, "Why don't you take yourself for a ride?" So, Lawrence did.

The Flying Junior that Lawrence sailed into a puff of wind ended up capsizing, but "I knew exactly what to do," he said. "I just climbed over the side, and I'm standing on the center board, trying to right the boat." The youngster simply wasn't carrying enough weight to right the ship, "but I wasn't panicked or anything."

That sense of calm in a storm would serve Lawrence, and a Singaporean sailor named Joseph Chan, extraordinarily well nearly three decades later.

While Lawrence remained cool-headed that day and waited

for his brothers to rescue him and bring him ashore, the incident raised his mom's blood pressure. Lawrence's mother, Margaret, who would go on to write a book about sailing in the area, yelled at him, "You're grounded for the summer!" She may not have really intended to enforce such a penalty, but she was determined Lawrence would be taught more of the ins and outs and finer points of sailing.

Lawrence, born on November 12, 1955, turned out to be quite a student of the sport. Often called Larry by fellow sailors and those he coached, he dove headlong into competitive sailing, which involves several types and classes of boats. They can range from single-handed boats such as the Finn or Laser class to a Tornado class catamaran for two sailors to keelboats like the Star, Yngling, or Etchells.

Over the years, Lawrence demonstrated a proficiency in sailing that propelled him to lofty heights. He represented his native Canada in the 1984 and 1988 Summer Olympics. He also won a Pan- American Games gold medal, coached in five other Summer Games, and trained athletes who appeared in several more. His country's sailing association named him the 1991 Canadian Male Athlete of the Year, and he subsequently was inducted into the Canadian Olympic Hall of Fame, the City of Edmonton Sports Hall of Fame, and the Alberta Sports Hall of Fame.

Despite the laurels and HOF recognitions, it was not the sailing itself but another act of valor that brought Lawrence to the pages of Wikipedia and this book. It was an irony not lost on either him or those closest to him. American Brian Ledbetter, a silver medalist in the Finn class in 1992, called his frequent training partner "a bulldog" who "hated to lose." Ledbetter added, "But he joked that the thing he was famous for was stopping and leaving a race."

Yet as I got to know Lawrence, I found out how committed he was to sailing, to finishing the race. Extremely proud of the sport, he was *immersed* in the beauty and the toil of it. Before I interviewed him, the first thing he sent me was a link to a seven-and-a-half-minute YouTube video from 2014 featuring Australian Finn sailor Oli Tweddell. The filmmaker of that video, Ben Hartnett, did a splendid job of introducing viewers to the rigors, the discipline, the weight training, and the incredible torque on the human body, which takes its toll on competitive

Going into the 1988 Summer Games, Lawrence Lemieux is "really confident" and believes it is his time for a medal. Credit: Courtesy Lawrence Lemieux

sailors who guide their vessels as they slap into the waves and fight the wind.

"You know, a lot of people don't realize it. They think of sailing as sitting in the back of the boat with a cocktail in your hand. Believe me, these athletes are fit," said Lawrence. He recalled a 1980s competition in New Zealand where the best athletes across a series of sports went head-to-head against one another. "So, there was somebody from rugby, soccer, all the different sports—and the sailor won the fitness thing."

For Lawrence, the tight fit with sailing and his love affair with the sport he plunged into for over a half century began in earnest when he was about fourteen years old. A few years later, he purchased a new Laser sailboat from a local dealer for $850, though he didn't have the money to pay for it. A friend agreed to loan him the money, tacking on 3 percent interest per month, requiring Lawrence to work numerous odd jobs to pay for the boat: pouring cement, hauling sheets of plywood, and more. It was a profound lesson in hard labor and in developing a work ethic that coursed through Lawrence's veins then and that centered him for years to come. "I can grind forever," he said. "People tell me I'm not very fast at the beginning, but then I get pretty fast at the end."

In pursuing sailing, Lawrence did what his older brothers had done, but more often and with more vigor than any of them had devoted to the sport. "He made a conscious decision to pursue it full-time, eight months of the year," his other older brother Ray said, whereas "I went to university and got married." Ray used to sail frequently with Lawrence and entered just about every regatta across Canada he could with his younger sibling. He and his brothers marveled at the gusto with which Lawrence threw himself into competitive sailing. "He went to these events, and he would go thousands of miles away. We were amazed at how good he became. In eight to ten years, he had left Edmonton and showed me and everyone else how good he was. He left us in the dust."

The allure of sailing to Lawrence comprised far more than the brute strength and speed required of the sport. "There's so many different tactics involved" that require the competitive sailor to constantly adjust and balance risk versus reward. "I found that really intriguing."

He meant "adjust and balance" figuratively, in a way, but mostly literally. "When sailing downwind in a big breeze, it's a bit like balancing a broomstick in your hand while skiing down a hill."

To say Lawrence found sailing "intriguing" is a colossal understatement. He passionately walked me through the strategic aspects of sailing, explaining to the novice that it's *these* components of the sport that often determine a winner. "Most sailors get wrapped up in trying to make the boat go faster by buying better equipment or sails. They look at it like a horse race rather than a chess match. As I was small in size for racing in the Finn class, it was difficult to keep up in the strong winds. I had to arrange my tactics and strategies to slow my competition down as opposed to going faster."

Lawrence was not the "fast in strong winds" competitor, nor was he, at 5'10" and 190 pounds, going to best his competition with size or weight. He learned to sail with an analytical mind and a mastery of the conditions at hand. Lawrence took me through a dictionary of sailing terms and tactics, explaining many of the things a competitor can do to impede his opponent's progress. One of them is "leebowing" a competitor, which is when sailors tack their boats from port to starboard as close as they can to get leeward of the other boat. That slows the opponent down due to the backwind coming off your sail and onto theirs. This usually makes the other boat tack away, which hopefully sends them in the wrong direction.

"Using the rules of sailing to your advantage is a major tactic," said Lawrence. "This is where the chess analogy comes in. You can put competitors into situations where they will lose speed or have to sail a longer distance. This is where real gains can be made."

He added that it's "better to win by an accumulation of small gains than looking to the one big gain. The thing is, the faster you go, the further you get off in the wrong direction. When it was really strong winds and I was not the fastest, I just needed to keep up. I needed to do better in the other guy's conditions than he does in mine. And my condition would be lighter winds. If I can finish in the top twenty in the strong winds and then win the lighter races, by the end of it, I'm doing really well."

Lawrence said he could go on for hours and hours describing these different scenarios. He anticipated them so well that he began to win local events. From there, he said, "I really wanted to see how far I could take it."

Thus began a nomadic existence that would take the Alberta-based athlete to the sailing havens of the world. Like the burgeoning soccer player who gravitates from pitch to pitch, Lawrence drove from race to race—except in his case, it would mean driving thousands of miles and leaving home for months on end. "I had a van that I put 400,000 to 500,000 miles on . . . and then I got another van." Altogether, he went through four of them, each one a Ford Econoline cargo van. "I lived in my van, pretty much full-time, from 1977 to 1990," he said.

The fact that Lawrence hailed from the province of Alberta made his slow-but-steady rise more impressive, said Dirk Kneulman, an Olympic and Pan Am games sailor, shipwright, boat builder, and world champion in the Etchells class who has known his close friend since the early 1970s. "You just don't see too many [elite] sailors come out of a small lake in Alberta that's frozen half the year. For him to compete . . . he lived a long way from everything."

Lawrence's journey up the ranks began with his first race outside Canada in 1975, at a Laser class US national event in Wichita. "I didn't know anyone and had no experience in a fleet that big and [with] sailors that good," he said. "I didn't finish great overall, but I won one race. That inspired me to keep going." Ray said his brother quickly ascended to the top of the Laser rankings in Alberta and then all of Canada.

Next, Lawrence worked all winter to get enough money to go to his first overseas event, the Laser World Championships in Germany, in 1976. There, he finished eighth overall out of 150 boats from all over the world and made good friends who would become instrumental to his future development. But there would be plenty more obstacles to overcome.

In 1976, Laser wasn't an Olympic class, but the Finn was. Canada hosted the 1976 Olympics in Montreal, and back then the host country supplied the Finn-class boats—in this case, fifty of them. After the Games, Canada gave those boats to sailors throughout the country, but Lawrence didn't get one, despite being a top sailor in the Laser class and on his way to getting into the Finn class.

Undaunted, Lawrence wrote the Canadian Yachting Association, which later became known as Sail Canada, pleading for a boat. There was one left—in a barn in Ontario, near the US-Canadian border. Lawrence drove 2,600 miles to Kingston to get the boat, only to discover that the reason no one else had claimed it was because it was not rigged. "It came with a bag of parts," he said. "Also, out of the fifty masts, there was only one left, presumably the one no one else wanted. I had no idea how to rig a Finn, so I then drove to Halifax, 1,500 miles farther east, and some friends there helped me rig it."

After sailing the vessel only a couple of times in Halifax, Lawrence wanted to try it out at the US Nationals in San Francisco. The boat went atop his van, and he drove 3,700 miles from Nova Scotia to the City by the Bay.

The vagabond sailor who drove across North America would soon gain respect from the veterans of sailing, but it was begrudgingly. Those US Nationals included some of the top sailors from Canada and the United States, including Olympians, and it began poorly for Lawrence. "I was still figuring out the rigging of my boat when the rest of the fleet had already left for the first race of the series. I ended [up] arriving at the start line with less than a minute to go before the start. As I approached the start line on port tack, my hiking strap slipped out of the cleat, and I fell out of the boat, but my feet were caught under the hiking strap."

He had no right-of-way over the starboard boats approaching the start line, but there was little he could do to change course. "I ended up fouling a couple boats . . . It pissed off some of the veterans who I overheard later saying, 'There are some guys out there who shouldn't be allowed to race against us.'"

Lawrence took his lumps, but he converted some of those same top sailors in 1978 when, sailing an old boat with a mast nobody else wanted, he finished fifth overall at his first Finn Class Gold Cup in Manzanillo. "Wow, you've really improved a lot," Lawrence heard from Ed Bennett, a 1972 Finn-class Olympian. Bennett was one of those who hadn't been quite as impressed with Lawrence in San Francisco, but now the positive feedback gave Lawrence a jolt of confidence, on the heels of that 1975 win in Wichita and that eighth-place finish in Germany. *I can* do *this,* he thought.

Two years later, in New Zealand, Lawrence made another breakthrough. He had broken his mast two days before another Finn Class

Gold Cup was to begin. "I found someone who could repair it, but the bend characteristics wouldn't be the same as before," he said. "I was told I was crazy to use that mast, as it would be slow and probably break." But he went ahead and used the repaired mast in the practice race the day before the Gold Cup began. "It didn't break, and my speed was fine, so I just used it for the entire event."

Lawrence ended up in third place overall at the championship but lamented that he should have won it. He had been ahead after five races despite piloting a patchwork quilt of equipment, but he made one big mistake that cost him the win. His late father, Leo, a semipro hockey player who was also very skilled at racquet sports, seized on that mistake and taught young Lawrence an important lesson when he returned home.

"What happened, did you get smart?" his dad asked. Leo was right; his son had outsmarted himself. Going into the sixth of seven races, Lawrence had changed his sail when there had been no need to. It led to him having his worst race of the series, and he ended up placing thirtieth in that individual event.

Ironically, though, all the sailing bumps and bruises and the cut-rate equipment trials and tribulations helped Lawrence perfect some of his tactical skills. He credited his dad with first instilling those in him. Before a game of Ping-Pong, Leo told his son he would spot him twenty points and then would beat him without scoring an attacking point. Come game time, that was exactly how it played out. Leo let young Lawrence make all the mistakes and capitalized on them.

Fatherly and other lessons learned, Lawrence continued to race and continued to beat others, rising to the top ranks in the world over the next dozen years. The stakes were getting higher—and then they reached well beyond the world of sport. In late 1979, Russia invaded Afghanistan. Canada and many other western nations joined the United States in boycotting the 1980 Olympic Games, and Lawrence was stung by the decision, which, as we learned, had also devastated a young American pole vaulter named Tom Hintnaus.

At the time, Lawrence was a "young, nonpolitical kid, not paying much attention to the news. I thought that it was sending a message to the Russian people that they're hosting a party and nobody is coming." Lawrence didn't necessarily agree, wryly recalling what he named his boat that year: "Just Pissing in the Wind," after the hit song by Jerry Jeff Walker.

While Lawrence's ship didn't sail in 1980, that Olympics no-show would be followed by four straight decades of Summer Games on which he left his fingerprints, either as an athlete, coach, or trainer, beginning with the 1984 Olympics. Lawrence's journey to those games was, he said, "a long story." He started off well enough but then began to burn out. The saga was about to end when he finished out of the running in the Finn class in the Olympic Trials. But then came a chance invitation when a Star class crew's helmsman withdrew from the Trials to get home to his pregnant wife.

Lawrence said the Star boat is one of the most complicated boats in the world to race because it requires many adjustments to the rig and sail, which can take years to master. He must have shown enough moxie in a test run, because the boat's owner asked Lawrence to race it in the Trials. However, a competitor named Michael Clements filed a protest, arguing the Star boat was not allowed to change helmsmen. "But it didn't specifically say that in the rules," Lawrence noted. "Two other boats changed *their* crew."

This created a dilemma for the Olympic Development Committee on two fronts: it had to decide what to do with the protest, and it had to determine what action to take against the Star boat Lawrence was about to pilot. It didn't appear the committee had a fair basis to allow other boats to change their crew but to disallow Lawrence replacing a helmsman. But the committee officials did worry about Lawrence's relative lack of experience on the Star boat and what might happen in the subsequent Olympic Games if Lawrence somehow pulled out the win.

So, Lawrence said, the Olympic Development Committee penalized his boat and put his team back in points "far enough that there was no way we could win." And yet they won their Trials competition—by less than one point. "No one expected I could possibly win with no experience in the Star boat."

At the 1984 Summer Games in Los Angeles, Lawrence's team finished in thirteenth place and enjoyed the satisfaction of having gone to the Olympics in Los Angeles. Clements never made it to the Olympic Games.

A year later, Lawrence returned to his beloved Finn class of racing. It was a class he excelled in, with nine career Finn Gold Cup top-ten finishes. He also had a 1991 European Championship win where he bested 1992 Olympic gold-medal-winner José van der Ploeg. His prowess in this class was especially remarkable because he was smaller and slighter than virtually all the men he competed against. "The Finn was the heavyweight boxing of sailing," said Ledbetter, who trained with Lawrence off and on between 1985 and 1992. "A lot of the best sailors in the world came from the Finn class, so it had the mystique. And it was usually big, strong guys [who competed]," Ledbetter added.

Leading up to the 1988 Olympics in Seoul, Lawrence began to figure it was *his* time. "Absolutely, I thought it was," he said. "I was really confident."

However, a series of unforeseen twists and turns put some pinpricks in that confidence. A major one was the stiff wind on September 24 in Pusan (a town later called Busan) that was nearly 200 miles from Seoul and that served as the home base for the Olympic sailing events. The conditions were the polar opposite of what they'd been the previous year, when Lawrence and other sailors had traveled to Pusan Bay for a pre-Olympic event and observed nary a wind at all. That was a prime reason the site was selected in the first place.

"We all assumed it would be the same in 1988," Lawrence said, but that day, "it turned out that was all wrong. It was really blowing, and on that particular day, it was howling." Lawrence was racing in the Finn class and was winning the race at the first mark. He was potentially en route to what would have been a much-needed win, especially since he had fallen off the pack in the first four days of racing, and this day marked the fifth of seven races for Finn-class competitors.

A half hour into the race, Lawrence couldn't see the six-foot-high fluorescent-orange mark number two due to the enormous size of the waves. "When you were in the trough of a wave, you couldn't even see the tip of the mast of a boat near you," he said. "It just worked out that every time I was on top of the wave, the marker was in the trough. I never saw it until it was too late." The runner-up sailor saw the orange marker before Lawrence did, passing him. That left Lawrence in second place.

But what Lawrence then *did* see would dramatically change his race, dictate a series of actions, and bend the arc of his career—or, at least, transform the way most nonsailors tend to remember him.

What Lawrence saw as he began the second of four windward legs was a capsized 470-class vessel, a helmsman hanging on to it, and then, away from the boat, a head bobbing in the water. The winds had grown even more severe to gale force by then, according to some reports. Lawrence could tell by the direction of the wind and the position of the boat that something was very wrong.

"In sailing, the rule of thumb is you always stay with the boat," Lawrence said. So, when he saw the head bobbing in the water away from the boat, he yelled to "ask them if they needed help." But through the noise of the wind and waves, no answer was forthcoming. This was Lawrence's moment in time, with a split-second decision at hand. He knew, with those conditions, that the odds for the fallen sailor were going to get much worse.

So, Lawrence chose to go beyond the racecourse boundary to rescue Joseph Chan, the Singaporean sailor. Chan was fortunate in more ways than one. First, Lawrence had somehow spotted him through the rising waves. Next, Lawrence had the strength to pull Chan out of the swirling waters. "I was able to grab the back of his life jacket and kind of just swung him into my boat," Lawrence said. And then Lawrence took it one step further.

Because the Finn class is a single-handed boat, Lawrence was in no position to take Chan with him, so he took Chan back to his capsized boat. There, Chan could be partnered back up with the other Singaporean sailor, Siew Shaw Her, whose hand was bleeding from the incident and who had done the correct thing by staying with the vessel. But Lawrence's rescue mission still was not complete. The two-man 470 was missing its rudder, so it couldn't be steered ashore.

After helping Chan back onto his boat, Lawrence knew he had to locate the boat's rudder. His analysis told him, "The rudder is going to be drifting upwind from where they were, it's white, and the water is blue. Serendipity, I guess—I found it." He took the rudder back to the 470. By then, sailing team coaches had observed the chaos and had been given permission, by the race committee, to go onto the course to help. Lawrence's coach, who had been looking for him, as he had been at the front of the race and now was nowhere to be seen, arrived at the capsized 470 just as Lawrence was returning the rudder.

Finally, Lawrence could go back onto the Finn-class course and rejoin the race, although his hopes of securing the win he needed had been dashed. He finished in twenty-second place out of twenty-three Finn-class boats that day, with nine other boats dropping out of the race entirely. Lawrence finished eleventh overall.

The rescue mission and the act of sportsmanship, however, convinced Olympic officials that Lawrence deserved much more. He ended up in a private ceremony with Juan Antonio Samaranch, president of the IOC, awarding him a special Pierre de Coubertin medal, also known as a True Spirit of Sportsmanship medal, a decoration given to those athletes, former and current, who by their actions exemplify the spirit of sportsmanship at the Olympic Games. Later, the International Yacht Racing Union decided to reinstate his position to what it had been when he went off course to rescue Chan, and he was awarded with a second-place finish for that race. These honors were awarded separately, and he did not displace the silver-medal winner for the Finn class.

While it seems hard to deny that Lawrence's actions on that day were heroic in nature, there were other perspectives on and reactions to what he did. Among the naysayers? Let's start with Lawrence himself.

A fierce competitor who took tremendous pride in what he accomplished as an athlete and a coach, Lawrence was also a lifelong sailor who had seen boats capsize time and time again. He said the credo among those in the sailing community is that if someone needs help, your job is to stop what you're doing and deliver that help.

But that wasn't the view of the Canadian media. Their attention had initially been fixated on Ben Johnson, the brash Canadian sprinter who won a gold medal in the 100 meters only to have it invalidated later by his steroid use. So the media's attention shifted from the alleged bad boy of the sprints to the Good Samaritan of the sailing competition.

The next morning as Lawrence made his way down to the boat park, a little later than usual, he discovered fifty to a hundred members

Lawrence Lemieux (in his white warmup jacket) does not win gold, silver, or bronze at the 1988 Summer Games. However, in honor of his courageous act, he is awarded a "True Spirit of Sportsmanship" medal. From left: International Yacht Racing President Peter Tallberg, International Olympic Committee President Juan Antonio Samaranch, and King Constantine of Greece. Credit: Lawrence Lemieux

of the press waiting for him. Lawrence the Finn-class sailor had to take a back seat to Lawrence the lifesaver. "I would have rather the press be there for my results rather than a rescue," Lawrence said. He felt the hype, the unyielding interview requests, and the ensuing loss of focus were as "detrimental" to his results as anything else. He would have preferred to attach a "no-big-deal" label to this rescue. And on whether he saved Chan's life, he said, "I've never thought about it in those terms. I would like to think somebody else would have done the exact same thing."

Paradoxically, the very fact that Lawrence saved Chan and received all those accolades triggered some mixed feelings within the sailing community. "There were some other athletes who didn't look favorably on" the press Lawrence received, said Chris Cook, a Finn-class sailor who has had a longtime athlete-to-coach relationship with Lawrence and has remained in close touch with him for two decades. "Other athletes felt he stole some of their glory and got all the attention." They felt the sailors winning the medals should have been the ones on the receiving end of the TV cameras and microphones. Still, Cook found the jealousy to be "kinda bs" and said Lawrence took critical steps at a critical time. "I don't think it was a *decision*. I think it is who he is. He is a compulsive helper, and he will always help people."

Cook also had an up-close and personal look at just how much Lawrence's actions meant to someone else: Chan. Serving as an extra and a driver on set for a series of McDonald's television commercials aired years later in which athletes from prior Olympics reenacted the events and scenes that made them famous, Cook was struck by the way Chan behaved around Lawrence on the set where the commercial was shot. While nobody can guarantee that Lawrence's efforts saved Chan's life, Cook said, "I'll tell you what I *did* see." Chan acted like a man who owed his life to Lawrence. "I've never seen anyone so happy to see another person," Cook shared. "He was showing Larry pictures of his kids, and you could tell he felt none of this would have happened without Larry's intervention."

Intervention is a good word to describe the two-decades-long coaching career Lawrence transitioned to after his competitive sailing days waned. Much like Lawrence the competitor, he was fiery and blunt as a coach. He brought his talents for strategy and tactics to his coaching and found a niche as the go-to coach for sailors who couldn't crack the top tier of their events. "A lot of guys I coached couldn't make the top twenty," he said. "I could get them near the top."

Cook became a shining example of that—eventually. He remembered, "In one of my first interactions with him in 2001, he and I had a battle. We had a little bit of a love-hate relationship." But that relationship matured into one of mutual respect, particularly after Cook saw what Lawrence was doing to help other athletes reach the Olympic Games in their class.

In 2004 to 2005, Cook began working with Lawrence in earnest, and Lawrence introduced him to the rigors of long-distance training. For five months, Cook would be in class at the University of Toronto Monday through Wednesday, and then he'd be on a flight to Fort Lauderdale to train with Lawrence Thursday through Sunday. "He saw something in me," said Cook, who rose from number thirty in the world to second at one point. "Larry's skill set was with the individual," Cook said. "He could do really great things with the individual that would buy in."

That routine was temporarily interrupted by a severe shoulder injury and subsequent surgery for Cook. But the Canadian system, and a sports psychologist Lawrence helped connect him with, enabled Cook to complete a difficult rehabilitation. Despite having his shoulder pop again prior to the 2005 World Championship in Moscow, Cook finished in third place in that event. The Lawrence-and-Cook partnership found even more success in 2008. Even after injuring his shoulder yet again, Cook ended up finishing in fifth place in the Finn class at the Beijing Olympics. He hadn't medaled, but the distance to the medal stand, he said, was "closer than it sounds, actually."

That knack for bringing out the best in sailing athletes reached well beyond Cook. Lawrence may not have coached his athletes to medal wins, but they were often on the front doorstep of attaining them. In 2016, Lawrence coached Robert Scheidt of Brazil, who finished fourth in the Laser class. Scheidt had garnered two prior Olympic gold medals, two silvers, and one bronze as a younger sailor, but when Lawrence worked with him, Scheidt was forty-three years old and well past his prime. Thus the fourth-place overall finish was considered a coup. That ability to get the most out of sailors is why several other previous Olympians, such as Juan Maegli of Guatemala, sought out Lawrence's help as well.

Ledbetter credits the Canadian with helping him get on the podium in the 1992 Barcelona Summer Games where Americans took home medals in nine out of ten sailing events. Lawrence did not emerge from the Olympic Trials that year, and he never officially coached Ledbetter. But the way Lawrence pushed him to the limit in training, Ledbetter recalled, "helped me win a medal. I give him a ton of credit."

Lawrence described himself as "a contract coach, not a federation coach." By that, he meant that he was most often asked to work with individuals as a private coach rather than serving as an official team coach. In large part, that was because Lawrence wasn't cut out for the politics that come with head coaching and national-team jobs. He preferred instead to tutor his athletes through no-nonsense candor, concentrated training, and the between-the-ears details of the sport.

That goes back to the strategic thinking Lawrence put into both competing and coaching, where he was adept at using maneuvers and rules in the wind to slow his competitors down, such as the leebow technique to force his opponents into a less favorable place on the racecourse, allowing him to minimize his errors and let others make them instead—and to embrace his philosophy of excelling, as he said, by "an accumulation of small gains, not just looking for that one big gain."

Lawrence said that all sports are equal when it comes to getting the most out of those you coach. "It is about being able to perform under pressure, and often you become more of a sports psychologist, keeping things in perspective and trying to prevent your athletes from making a stupid mistake." It's that kind of frankness that defined Lawrence as both a competitor and a coach. The question is whether Lawrence may have been a bit *too* candid, too wrapped around the "tell it like it is" approach.

"He's pretty honest," said Kneulman. "I wouldn't call it rude, but he's honest." Added older brother Ray, "He didn't like to take lip from anyone. He would always call 'em out."

Cook said that in part resulted in other top Canadian sailors, such as Hank Lammens, receiving "favorite child" status with Sail Canada rather than Lawrence, even though their skills and abilities were closely matched.

He may not have been winning popularity contests, but Canada's elite sailors knew that to be the best, they had to beat the best—and for many years, the top target was Lawrence. "Hank would be one of the first to say that to get to where he got, he needed to beat Lawrence," said Kneulman. "To get to that level, you have to beat those at the highest level."

Nearly fifty years after he entered the arena of competitive sailing, Lawrence continued to remain true to himself. His sailing career extended to a seniors circuit, where he captured five World Masters Championships as well as one third-place and two second-place finishes. He also has remained comfortable in his own skin, funny, engaging, and proud of what he has done. As Kneulman put it, those who truly know the sport of sailing also know Lawrence should be defined for his sailing ability, not for that rescue act. "He's been a great competitor, a great coach. He's had lots of setbacks, but he got back up and kept on going. That's what a great athlete does."

Ledbetter, who grew up sailing in the San Diego Yacht Club and has enjoyed great success in sailing, labeled Lawrence as "one of the smartest, craftiest sailors out there." He said he and Lawrence regularly traded back and forth between first and second place in events and championships between 1985 and 1992. "He was really fast downwind and really good in the light air, and he had all those tools in the toolbox."

That toolbox, and that status as a "compulsive helper," enabled Lawrence to spot Chan in the raging waves of Pusan that September 1988 day and ensured the Singaporean sailor could end up not just as the guy whose boat capsized but also as the guy who rose to become head of training and development for the Singapore Sailing Federation.

While Lawrence will downplay the incident for the rest of his days, others won't. "That guy was in trouble," Kneulman explained. Ledbetter said rescues of capsized boaters may be common and par for the course in sailing but are more of a rarity in the middle of an Olympic race, where competitors are uber-focused on the prize.

"The sailboat is going one way, and the other guy is going upwind and into the current," Ledbetter said. Chan was drifting farther away and would soon have been a few football fields from his boat. "At that point, you're searching for a dot in the ocean," he said. "I think there's a high likelihood that guy wouldn't have been found if a competitor on the racecourse had not stepped in."

PART IV

FACING RACISM

CHAPTER 10

MEL WAKABAYASHI, JAPAN

MEN'S HOCKEY (NATIONAL TEAM COACH), 1980 WINTER OLYMPICS, LAKE PLACID

Hockey- and baseball-playing savant Hitoshi "Mel" Wakabayashi stood only 5'6" tall. But chat up those who knew and loved him, and you will hear about a true giant.

A flip through Mel's life story is a view of a fairy-tale journey in many respects. He spent his eight decades reaching the pinnacle of most everything he tried. Multisport star as a kid. Legendary Canadian baseball and hockey player in Chatham, Ontario, and a 2005 inductee into the Chatham Sports Hall of Fame. Two-sport standout at the University of Michigan and a 2006 inductee into the university's Hall of Honor. Named by the Western Collegiate Hockey Association (WCHA) in February 2002 as one of its top fifty players in fifty years. Hockey-playing and coaching icon in Japan, who led the country's national team in the 1980 Olympics. President of Seibu Canada. Vice president of the Japan Ice Hockey Federation. Married for more than fifty years to his wife, Suzuko.

Look deeper, though, because Mel's life was also about overcoming a series of challenges and obstacles in his path. He had to overcome doubts about his size and, perhaps more importantly, his heritage. He was born into a Japanese-Canadian internment camp in British Columbia, his parents suffering the same cruel and inhumane fate that thousands of other Japanese Americans and Japanese Canadians did after World War II erupted. Racism, mostly subtle but sometimes overt, crept into Mel's amateur and professional career.

Let's start with the internment camps, because that is where Mel spent the first seven years of his life. I never got the chance to learn from him how much he remembered about growing up in an internment camp as a young boy, but his older sister by a couple of years, Shirley Takahashi, shared some of what she recalled. Anti-Japanese sentiment in Canada, including violence and riots, can be traced back to the early 1900s, when Japanese immigrants first arrived in significant numbers. Then, during World War II, all Japanese Canadians were required to register with the Canadian government, and some were accused of being spies. Some 21,000 Japanese Canadians were forcibly removed from their homes and ordered off fishing boats without any due process, and many were incarcerated in abandoned homes and makeshift shacks, most of which were located in the province of British Columbia.

Shirley remembered that her mom and dad "left everything but the few things that fit in a couple suitcases for themselves and three little toddlers. Many families lost their homes as well as their properties." In addition to the camps in British Columbia, there were another seven hundred Japanese Canadians transported to prisoner-of-war camps in Ontario after resisting evacuation orders.

If that oppression marked Mel's early years, then devastating diseases after a lifetime of very good health marked his final one. His son Chris said it began with a rare heart disease in January and February of 2023, but Mel seemed to have slapshot that one away. Next came a more formidable opponent: a tumor in his liver and colon cancer, which not even the finest of athletes could overcome. "It was like someone hit you with a baseball bat," said Chris, who had followed his dad's footsteps into coaching hockey in Japan. The person Chris most emulated, the father who "made me what I am," the fierce competitor who faced down nearly every athletic foe, died at age eighty, on July 9, 2023.

Mel Wakabayashi's hockey playing prowess at the University of Michigan leads the Detroit Red Wings to draft him—and he played for two of the club's minor-league teams. Credit: Bentley Historical Library, Bentley Image Bank / University of Michigan

In between those early years and his final one, Mel's life was a rich blend of quiet heroism, of actions speaking loudly, and of accomplishments across athletic and corporate sectors. "I'm very proud that I can say Mel Wakabayashi was a friend of mine," said Paul Allen, a teammate of Mel's, along with Hall-of-Fame pitcher Fergie Jenkins, on the Chatham Bantams baseball team. Allen went on to author two books, including *Bright Lights Black Stars*, a profile of Negro League players and Canada's oldest baseball league. Allen likened Mel's influence in Canada and Japan to hockey great Gordie Howe, who "always had time for an autograph and made everyone feel better about themselves. I think our good buddy Mel was like that."

As prolific an athlete as Mel was in Canada and at the University of Michigan, his most profound impact on sporting life may have been in Japan, where Mel and his younger brother Herb took the game of hockey to a new level. "When he came over [to Japan], people were saying, 'Who is this guy?' They couldn't believe what they were seeing," Chris said. Mel had an arsenal of moves that just weren't in the Japanese hockey lexicon at the time, such as the slapshot and the way he was using his backhand. "So, I guess he had a huge impact."

The Wakabayashis were fabulous skaters and stickhandlers who could think rapidly and were therefore instrumental in upping the quality of hockey in Japan, said Ian Kennedy, an Ontario native and author who founded the online Chatham-Kent Sports Network and wrote about the hurdles athletes like Mel faced in his 2022 book, *On Account of Darkness: Shining Light on Race and Sport*. He said Mel and Herb "played the game of hockey we love today years prior to that."

Mel spent years developing his skills and talents as a sports-crazy kid. His coming-of-age years were in Chatham, which lies about an hour's drive north of the US-Canada border. The Chatham-Kent metro area has a population of over 104,000, but Chatham appeared to have had only 30,000 to 40,000 people when the Wakabayashis arrived in 1950. It wasn't long after that Mel and his seven siblings played and excelled in an array of athletic activities.

Mel and Herb, who went on to have his own starring role in Canadian and Japanese hockey and his own place in the Olympics, would play in their driveway for hours on end. They lived on Degge Street, along with another kid Herb's age, Eddie Wright, who would also go on to have a sterling hockey career as a player, coach, and scout. Wright recalled fond memories of those days in the Wakabayashi driveway. "In the summer, it would be pitcher-catcher-hitter, and in the winter, it would be goalie-defenseman-forward," he said. "We put in 10,000 hours [playing on that driveway]."

For Wright, the attachment to Mel and Herb went beyond sports. His dad died when he was six years old, so the Wakabayashis became a second family to him. "Herb and I were attached at the hip," but it was Mel, Herb's elder by two years, whom Wright idolized. "Mel was my hero, the guy I aspired to want to be like. He was bigger than life, just excelled at everything he touched."

"He was a good golfer, too," quipped Shirley, the third of the eight Wakabayashi kids and herself a high school softball, basketball, and volleyball player who still bowled well enough to have earned a perfect score in five-pin decades later. She added that older brother Don was a top-flight minor-league hockey player for the Chatham Senior Maroons as well.

Shirley said that despite the athletic accolades Mel and most of his siblings received, they remained soft-spoken and humble—a behavior modeled by their parents. Mel's father, Tokuzo, worked at a cosmetics factory, and the family had a side business cooking tofu out of their garage. "Mom and Dad were very quiet, private people, and my brothers didn't say a whole lot, either," Shirley said.

Of course, here is where Theodore Roosevelt's famous advice to "speak softly and carry a big stick" comes into play. Mel, an accomplished all-around athlete, made his sticks of choice the ones you find on a baseball field and a slab of ice. And, as adept as Mel was in a hockey arena, the stories of what he did on the baseball fields of Ontario and the University of Michigan are stacked high and wide as well.

Ed Robbins played all-star baseball with both Mel and Jenkins. He shared that, at least initially, Mel's star shone brighter than that of Jenkins. Robbins played first base and Mel second base for those all-star teams, and "Mel came in right away as first-string," Robbins said. "He was very quiet—let his play speak for him. We called him 'Squeak.'"

Robbins, who went on to a nearly four-decade-long career as a teacher, school superintendent, and board of education official, still vividly remembered a particular game against a team from Niagara where "Squeak's" performance screamed rather loudly. The game went fifteen innings, but it was on the verge of ending in the ninth inning when Niagara had runners on first and second base with nobody out. It was then that a Niagara player bunted, and Mel "charged the bunt and caught it and started a triple play," Robbins said. Then, in the bottom of the fifteenth, Mel came up and hit a scorching line drive that "careened off the second baseman's leg and into the outfield." That was all the speedy Mel needed to turn the game into a walk off. "He came all the way around and scored."

Told of Robbins's story, Allen remarked, "Let's just say that was not the first time Mel Wakabayashi made great plays or had crucial hits." He recalled a game where Mel batted leadoff and the opposing team's outfielders moved very shallow, erroneously judging Mel's power by his size. "He hit it over their heads."

The hits kept coming after Mel arrived at the University of Michigan, too. Wright distinctly remembered a time when he and Herb were home on a break from school and drove to watch Mel's Michigan team play against rival Michigan State University. "He hit a home run to the deepest part of the park," Wright said, with a shake of his head. "It was unbelievable."

Mel was a talented-enough player in Ontario and at Michigan that the nearby Detroit Tigers took notice, inviting him to their training camp as a potential second baseman for their minor-league system. But in those days, Allen said, many second basemen were bigger guys, and Mel thus did not see baseball as his path forward.

"Baseball was my favorite—I got better coaching at a young age," Mel wrote. But he didn't think he was an elite player. "I just enjoyed the game."

Hockey was another matter. "People around me urged me to play in the [National Hockey League (NHL)]," Mel indicated. No wonder. As a hockey player, "Mel out-quicked you and outsmarted you," according to Wright. In one particular year, Mel played only half a season for the Chatham Junior Maroons and still won the scoring championship with a whopping fifty goals.

Name an honor at Michigan and with the WCHA, and chances are Mel earned it. Two goals in the NCAA championship game in 1964 to help Michigan win the title. First-team All-America in 1964–65 and winner of the WCHA scoring title. Leading scorer for Michigan in his junior and senior seasons. Team captain. WCHA Most Valuable Player in the 1965–66 season.

Mel ultimately enjoyed a high-profile career for Michigan in *both* hockey and baseball. His secret weapons on a baseball diamond were his speed and his all-around skill, both at the plate and in the field.

And on the ice? As his lifelong friend Wright pointed out, it was that combination of quickness, elusiveness, speed, and smarts. After Mel passed away, his Michigan teammates and fellow Chatham natives took note of all those attributes in an effusive obituary published in Chatham's local paper.

"He was on the small side, but they really couldn't touch him," said one of those teammates, Al Hinnegan, in that obituary. "He had so many good moves." In the same obituary, another Michigan teammate and fellow Chatham native, Ron Coristine, recalled the embarrassment for one defender who experienced Mel's shiftiness firsthand. "[He] looked at Mel and thought he was going to rock him into the next seats. Mel made a couple of moves on him and left part of his equipment in the rafters and went by him. It was unbelievable." With the phrase "left part of his equipment in the rafters," Coristine was referring to Mel's ability to fake an opponent way out of position—or what many male athletes have crudely termed "faking a guy out of his jockstrap." Coristine added, "You might think you were going to have him lined up for a pretty solid check, but he was just as elusive as you'd want to be. Give you a head fake one way, and he'd be going the other. He was great."

The NHL's Detroit Red Wings, playing in close proximity to the Wolverines' Ann Arbor campus, knew plenty about Michigan's high-octane goal scorer. Mel signed with the Red Wings and spent the 1966–67 season in Detroit's minor-league system, playing with Memphis in the central league and Johnstown in the eastern league. But before the start of Detroit's next training camp, an opportunity knocked on Mel's door, one that would change the curvature of his life and the fortunes of hockey in Japan—but also one that would leave a potential NHL career in the rearview mirror.

In the Far East, through the efforts of billionaire businessman and real-estate investor Yoshiaki Tsutsumi, officials were starting up a Japan Ice Hockey League. Tsutsumi had inherited his father's successful business, the Seibu Corporation, which was a holder of railways, hotels, and more. As chairman of the Japan Ice Hockey Federation, Tsutsumi instinctively knew he needed star power to ensure the success of the new league. He saw just that in Mel, who was part of the first wave of hockey players recruited to the fledgling league.

To hear several close friends and family members tell it, the emissary who helped recruit Mel was Father David Bauer, a former Canadian ice-hockey player tabbed by Tsutsumi to suggest players and coaches to bring to Japan. They said another recruiter for Tsutsumi was Father Bob Moran. Kennedy pointed to former NHL player John "Peanuts" O'Flaherty.

Whomever the recruiter was, he succeeded. Mel journeyed to Japan, where he suited up for the Seibu Railway Hockey Team in 1967 and successfully convinced the team a year later to add Herb. Mel would go on to play for twelve years in Japan and later became Tsutsumi's president of Seibu Canada, tending to Seibu's hotels in Toronto and elsewhere. Just as he had targeted Mel for his hockey prowess, Tsutsumi trusted Mel's business acumen as well. He asked Mel to oversee his properties throughout the world and especially in Canada.

As his playing career wound down in the late 1970s, Mel found something else he could do very well in the game of hockey: coach. Chris said his father was a big believer in instilling mental skills along with physical tools. Mel also brought to Japan the idea of conditioning, making his players run during practice when that was virtually unheard of. It even made his son wonder. "I once asked him, 'Why did you make your guys run so much, like they're a track team?'" But, said Chris, it was part of his dad's genius. "Those were just things he ingrained—it was the mental-toughness part of what he did."

Mel's coaching chops earned him the nod to lead Japan's national team in the 1980 Olympics. The kid born into the horrors of an internment camp had graduated to the wonders of strolling through an Olympic Village in Lake Placid for the Winter Games, and Mel described it as "the most amazing experience in my life . . . a dream come true. Entering the Olympic Stadium and being able to feel the energy in the crowd was unbelievable."

Shirley remembered the 1980 Olympic experience well, too. She and their parents were there to watch brother Mel coach in the games and brother Herb play in them. "It was a very exciting time." Herb, who passed away in 2015, carried the flag for Japan in the 1980 opening ceremonies and ended up playing in three Olympics overall.

It would be tempting here to write about glorious heights reached by that 1980 Japan team, but it would also be mythology. Chris characterized the national team's status at that time as more of a B-pool-level squad, and the scores from Lake Placid reinforced that. While the United States would celebrate a massive "Miracle on Ice" upset win over Russia, Japan would be on the other end of a 16–0 rout at the hands of the Soviets. The Japanese also lost 6–0 to Canada, 5–1 to Poland, and 6–3 to Finland, though they did manage a tie with the Netherlands.

Given Mel's undeniable brilliance in Chatham and at the University of Michigan, and the decision by the nearby Detroit Red Wings to sign him, one might wonder about his choice to eschew the opportunity to play in the world's finest hockey league in favor of being a trailblazing tone-setter for an unproven one. Did he have regrets about the decision to leave for the start-up league? Could he have helped create a path to NHL ice rinks for himself and other ultra-talented players of color like Herb and Wright?

Mel's thoughts were mixed on this topic. On the one hand, he wrote that looking back, he had "lots of regrets" and "not enough confidence" about cracking an NHL roster. But he also indicated he wanted to explore his Japanese heritage and that he "wanted to prove we could win a championship with a new team."

The reality check for Mel, his younger brother, and Wright was that the NHL was—and remains—overwhelmingly Caucasian in composition. There are a variety of perspectives regarding the presence and extent of racism in hockey, as well as baseball and all sports generally, and how directly it has impacted and undermined elite athletes of color. Kennedy devoted hours of research into this topic, interviewing Wright, among others. "We have a way to go in terms of people recognizing the barriers they *did* face," Kennedy said. In his book and in our interview, he referenced Wilfred "Boomer" Harding, a Chatham-born baseball and hockey luminary who played in the decade before Mel and who, in 1945, was turned away at the door of the old Olympic Stadium in Detroit, where "public skating meant whites only."

It is difficult to discern what role race may have played in Mel's family decision to head for Japan. Chris noted that one factor influencing his dad was the fact that only the "original six" NHL franchises existed when Mel was weighing a North American career versus a

*From left: Herb Wakabayashi, Mel Wakabayashi, and Eddie Wright of the Junior Maroons
Hockey Club in Chatham, Ontario. Credit: Nikkei National Museum*

Japanese one, which meant fewer career opportunities overall. An expansion to twelve teams came soon after, and today's NHL is stocked with thirty-two teams.

It is also important to juxtapose modern-day race relations—which remain rocky—with what existed in the United States and Canada overall in the 1950s and 1960s of Mel's era. Both countries were less than a decade removed from the internment camps of World War II. Discrimination in employment, race riots, and inhumane treatment of non-Caucasians were very real. The Wakabayashis and Wright likely saw "the handwriting on the wall as to who looked like them [in the NHL]," Kennedy said. "There was almost nobody." They may very well have harbored genuine doubts as to whether the league was exclusively "where people with the best skills would have been welcomed. And we're still dealing with that today."

That said, the Chatham area of the 1950s and 1960s did seem to be ahead of its time when it came to race relations—at least with the teams of the day. That is more significant given the tiny sliver of the Chatham-Kent population that was of South Asian or Southeast Asian descent. While an exact census from those decades is difficult to locate, the modern-day Asian population is still less than 2 percent. Robbins, who is African Canadian, said he remembered only a couple of instances of racial taunting and the "N" word on the baseball diamond, and the Chatham teams dealt with it by banding together and letting the power of their performance do the talking. "In both cases," he said, "we beat the other team so badly. The whole team melded together, and we beat the other team unmercifully." Allen said he "never except one time saw any incidents of racial taunting." He pointed with pride to how the Chatham squads of his day, and the parents that watched them, formed a sort of "United Nations of baseball teams . . . Their parents and my parents stood up for each other. We would turn the other cheek, and we would say to our teammates, 'We'll back you up.'"

Still, there is simply no getting around the degrading race-baiting that reared its ugly head from time to time. "It was mainly name-calling," Shirley said. The Wakabayashis would typically be called a combination of "Japs" or "slant eyes" or "chink" or "chinky chinky Chinamen," displaying both bigotry and ignorance, considering her brothers were of Japanese, and not Chinese, heritage. Interestingly, Chris said his dad sometimes received a cold shoulder from fans after he moved to Japan, because they didn't think he was truly one of *their* native Japanese sons.

One of the many gifts the Wakabayashi brothers possessed on the ice was to ignore the outside noise. "Mel and Herb did not react—they learned that early on," Wright said. By contrast, he found it extremely difficult to let the racist moments pass, especially when the "N" word was used in one of his junior-league games. "I dropped the gloves," he said, ready to fight. "It took me a lot of years to learn that if you don't react, then the problem was theirs, not yours."

Another quality of Mel's that is cited by those who knew, played with, and grew up with him was his humility. "So soft-spoken, so humble, no braggart in him. That stood out to me," Robbins said. Mel's nephew Dwight Wakabayashi, who idolized his uncle, said Mel combined that modesty with a penchant for well-chosen words to keep others humble and to remind them that it all started with hard work and dedication. His uncle would always ask how school and hockey were going and tell him, "You better get your homework done before you shoot some pucks."

Dwight said he was a pretty good player as a youngster, but added, "Uncle Mel always liked to put me in my place." He remembered a particular game when he was fourteen or fifteen, and his team was in the all-Ontario finals. His uncles Mel and Herb were both in the stands to watch. His team won, but Dwight had a rough game. Afterward, Mel had a few words for him. "I have heard so much about you and what a player you are . . . Well, I've got to tell you, I'm not impressed." Dwight *knew* he'd had a crappy game. "You were not going to get any sugar-coating from him, and I loved that about him. You want that, right?" Dwight has credited his uncles as being instrumental in his successful bid to make a junior-hockey team in British Columbia for the 1992–93 season. As a journalist, Dwight has also written about the top fifteen Chatham Junior Maroons hockey players of all time, and, unsurprisingly, both his uncles made the list.

Members of Mel's inner circle talked on and on about his incandescent talents as an athlete. They also conveyed how much they revered him, even though most of their face-to-face interactions with him became more sporadic given that Mel spent over a half century of his life based in Japan. As he thought back on his youth with Mel and Herb, Wright noted that he was "a very, very fortunate individual to have grown up where I did." Of Mel, he said, "I would do anything for that individual." He also couldn't resist sharing a wisecracking exchange he and Mel traded years ago when Wright sent his friend a birthday card addressed to "Squeak." Mel had a ready message in return for his 5'3" buddy: "You'll always be a pebble—too small to be a rock."

On a serious note, Wright learned some lifelong lessons from Mel, Herb, and the Wakabayashis that he wished a younger generation would latch onto more often. One of them was the value of working your tail off. "One summer, we loaded boxcars with 114-pound bags of flour. It seemed like the harder we worked together, the more fun we had."

Chris, who has coached for nineteen years at the top levels of Japanese hockey, started coaching the same Kokudo team his dad once coached and later rose to take over the helm of the Tohoku Free Blades. He couldn't get very far without being reminded of the pedestal his father stood on in the eyes of so many people. When an auto-insurance broker saw the name "Wakabayashi," he asked Chris if Mel was his dad. Assured that he was, the insurance broker responded, "He's my idol." Said Chris: "I feel a lot of pride in my dad; I'm really grateful for him to have been my dad."

Kennedy harkened back to the sportsmanship and class the Wakabayashis displayed in the community. "They were really beloved—the whole family." In that same vein, Shirley, who settled in Chatham and spent forty-four years as a teacher, said she is perhaps proudest of the positive imprint her brothers have had on nephews, grandkids, and those throughout the community, even decades after they moved across the world. "Anytime I go anywhere, when people hear the name Wakabayashi, they are just very proud of what [her brothers] have done."

An on-the-surface inspection of what Mel did might not lead you straight to the term *hero*. He missed out on an NHL career. His Japan national team took its lumps in that 1980 Olympics in Lake Placid. Across its participation in twenty-two Winter Olympic Games, the country has never medaled in ice hockey. And hockey still struggles to find footing in Japan versus sports like soccer, baseball, basketball, rugby, and more.

But maybe, once again, we need to rightsize how we define *heroism*. Mel earned lifelong respect and awe from those who knew and played with him. He and Herb made Japanese hockey significantly better than it would have been without their skating and playmaking abilities. His countrymen chose him to lead the Japanese national team. He became a top and trusted executive at Seibu. He built a family and passed on to his son the love of the game he felt so fortunate to have played. Moreover, Mel demonstrated to those who hurled racist taunts that their words were harming *themselves*, not he nor his family. He did that, as Wright noted, by never giving them the power to see that their words had any impact whatsoever. *That* was far more potent than fighting back or trading taunts ever could be.

The beautiful thing about Mel's story is that hockey started as a game in his driveway but turned into so much more. In his final days, he had a chance to write about his life and the driving force for all the incredible opportunities he received, and he described himself as a simple Japanese boy growing up in Chatham, Ontario, who loved the game of hockey. "Hockey took care of me physically, mentally, and financially . . . Hockey is my life. Without hockey, I wouldn't have [had] my dreams come true."

CHAPTER 11

PETER NORMAN, AUSTRALIA

200 METERS, 1968 SUMMER OLYMPICS, MEXICO CITY

When the moment in time came to decide what was right, Peter Norman chose human rights.

Peter Norman? To knowledgeable sports fans and Olympic Games aficionados, it is a name that will ring the faintest of bells—if it rings one at all. Understandable on one hand, yet sad on the other.

It has been over a half century since Peter first won acclaim as a guy who could run very, very fast. No Australian before or since has covered 200 meters in less time than he did on a high-altitude Mexico City track in 1968. The Summer Olympics that year was actually held in the autumn in October to capitalize on more comfortable Mexico City temperatures. Peter's story unfolded on October 16, just four days before a Tanzanian marathoner profiled earlier in this book, John Akhwari, would endure a mighty struggle to overcome injuries and finish an Olympic marathon.

The fame Peter received for his sprint to the finish and the silver medal it earned him is not the distressing part of his journey. Instead, it's the sorrowful lack of awareness of Peter's role *after* the race concluded. Many people recall, or have heard about, Tommie Smith and John Carlos on the 200-meter medals stand, their dark-gloved hands raised skyward in salute to Black power and human rights. The pose remains to this day a powerful symbol of the fight for racial equality. Unfortunately, often forgotten or overlooked are Peter's ideas and actions, depicting him as a vital civil rights trailblazer who stood with Smith and Carlos.

"In a way, his story is more important than Tommie and John's," said Matt Norman, Peter's nephew.

Peter's story is also a complex one. There is little in dispute about what he did on that October day and why it mattered. The stuff of disagreement lies in what happened to him afterward, what treatment he received, and how long it took for him to be duly recognized. Sadly, the debate has endured without Peter's own voice; he died of a heart attack in 2006. It has since been left to others to dissect the details and to determine, in their own minds, whether or how much Peter suffered for his actions at that Mexico City medals ceremony.

Twenty-six years earlier, Peter was born on June 15, 1942, in the town of Coburg, a suburb of Melbourne. He was the firstborn son of George and Thelma Norman, who ultimately raised a family of four kids.

During that era, the Salvation Army organization was very popular in Australia and placed a significant focus on teaching people Christian values. The organization also promoted the values of compassion, of treating all others as equals, and of helping those in need without discrimination. Peter's parents passed on to him the same Salvation Army ethos that had been passed on to *them* by their parents, and it played a very influential part in Peter's life and on his actions on a Mexico City medals podium.

When it came to sprinting, Peter got an atypically late start. He lacked a serious tutor and ran in borrowed spikes until a legendary Athletics Australia coach, Neville Sillitoe, spotted him running alone on a track. Peter's sprint career, and correspondingly his times, took off after he joined Sillitoe's East Melbourne Harriers for the 1961–62 season.

We know these sorts of details in part from the compelling 2008 documentary *Salute*, a film produced by Matt, who founded Wingman Pictures. "Peter was like a father figure to me," said Matt, whose own father, Laurie, was the second child in the Norman family, born nearly four-and-a-half years after his big brother. "It was one of the reasons I made the film, because he was a hero to me." While *Salute* was a posthumous tribute, Matt had started working on it while his uncle was still alive, so Peter, as well as both Smith and Carlos, took part in it and are quoted extensively.

Matt also assisted Andrew Webster with the writing of *The Peter Norman Story* and Damian Johnstone with the writing of *A Race to Remember*. He said these works were also an homage to his uncle. Still, while a documentary and two books regarding Peter made the rounds Down Under, there is only a hazy awareness outside his native Australia regarding his life and his human-rights actions. It is why, in my mind, his story flew under the radar. Only a small fraction of track-and-field devotees knew much about him.

Of course, one woman who knew plenty about Peter was Ruth Newnham, who fell in love with him and became his first wife. After the couple married and began to build a life together, Janita Norman, was the firstborn of Peter's three kids from that initial marriage. She said that although her father wasn't home a lot, "Dad was always fun and doing adventurous things." She loved to tag along with her pop, recalling, "I would go with him to the track while he trained." Janita remembered her dad, too, as a great cook who would make dishes like spaghetti Bolognese for the family.

Over the years, Janita said, her father was "always at the forefront of change—pushing the boundaries." Unfortunately, she lost much of her regular face time with her dad at age five when Peter and Ruth divorced. Looking back, a part of Janita wishes she had sought out a long conversation with him while he was still alive. "It's one of my regrets that I didn't," she said. "It would be a damn interesting conversation."

From all accounts, Peter was a damn interesting guy. In *The Peter Norman Story*, which recounted Peter's roller-coaster journey, his early-adult lifestyle included church, youth groups, netball, theater, and track and field. The sprinting part of Peter's sporting life didn't take center stage until after the fateful meeting with Sillitoe, but once it did, it became clear Athletics Australia had a unique talent on its

America's gold and bronze medalists Tommie Smith (center) and John Carlos (right) raise their arms in a "Black Power" gesture during a medal ceremony in the 1968 Olympic Games in Mexico City. Both men wore a black glove on one raised hand with fist clenched as the US flag was raised. Peter Norman from Australia (left) won the silver medal. Credit: Smith Archive / Alamy

hands. Only a year after he began training with his coach, Peter finished sixth in the 220-yard dash semifinals at the Commonwealth Games in Australia.

Two years later, an ankle injury dashed Peter's hopes of making the Australian national team for the 1964 Tokyo Olympics. But a breakthrough came in 1966, when he won a national championship in the 200 meters in 20.9 seconds, besting fellow sprinters Greg Lewis and Gary Holdsworth, who had previously competed in the 100-, 200-, and 4×100-meter relays for Australia at the 1964 Summer Games. Peter won another national title in the 200 in 1967.

When it came time for the 1968 Summer Games, at the nearly one-and-a-half-mile-high (7,350 feet) altitude of Mexico City, Peter and Lewis had made the Australian Olympic team while Holdsworth narrowly missed out. Both Australian sprinters ran well in their heats at the Games and into the semifinals for the 200 meters, but Lewis just missed making the finals. Peter, who had clocked a blazing 20.2 in one of his races, was in.

The 200-meter final became one of the fastest in history. Smith, the winner, set a world record, and Peter, the runner-up, set what has remained as the Australian national record. He did so after the Australia's team manager persuaded him that a Lane 6 assignment for the finals could work to his advantage. The team manager was right. It did.

Peter had a well-deserved reputation as a slow starter with a freight-train-fast finish, and he joked about it in *The Peter Norman Story*. "I would have found it very hard to beat my grandmother out of the starting blocks," he said. He described being sixth in the eight-man field as the sprinters entered the final straightaway—and the mistake Carlos made by looking around too much. "When he [Carlos] turned into the straight, he was a gold medalist, but Tommie went past him as if he was standing still at the top of the straight." And then Peter showed off the fast finish for which he was known.

At the tape, Smith had won in a world-record 19.83. Peter, brandishing that fearsome finishing kick, took silver in 20.06 seconds. Carlos had run a dazzling but unofficial 19.7 in a pre-Olympics event, but on this day he settled for bronze in 20.10 seconds. The times were aided by the thin air of high altitude, but they would still be considered very fast in the *modern-day* track-and-field era—let alone in 1968. Smith's world record would remain intact for eleven years.

After the race, other runners referred to Peter's relative lack of name recognition. American Larry Questad, who had finished sixth after envisioning a USA sweep, was quoted as saying, "Peter came from nowhere. I'd never come across his name." Smith, however, brushed past that and put the Australian's race in the proper perspective: "He didn't need fanfare before he got there. He just ran *fast.*"

All this rehashed race drama sounded—and was—scintillating. But it paled in comparison to what happened leading up to and during the 200-meter medals ceremony. And here's the thing: Peter, the 5'9" white guy who finished in between two African American sprinters, ran to the center of it all.

To foreshadow the importance of what Peter did on the walk up to and on the medals podium, it is helpful to dial back to what had preceded the 1968 Summer Games. African American leaders had threatened a boycott of the Summer Games; after all, racial tensions had boiled in the months since Martin Luther King Jr., the civil rights icon who preached of achieving progress through nonviolent protests, had been assassinated on a motel balcony in Memphis. While the boycott was called off, civil rights leader Harry Edwards did orchestrate a series of protests to elevate the cause of racial equality at those 1968 Olympics. The plan was for Smith and Carlos, both Black men, to be two of the key baton-carriers for spotlighting the need for racial justice in front of an Olympic-size crowd.

Peter pumped more fuel into the effort. A few minutes after his legs took him 200 meters in just over 20 seconds, Peter made rapid-fire decisions with his conscience and his mind. Taken together, they screamed "human rights ambassador" much louder than "fastest white guy in the world."

Years later, in *Salute*, he referenced what Carlos had said—that "the three of us were put on this Earth to do a job." Peter believed that third spot, next to Smith and Carlos, "was destined to be me." It was Peter who had learned of the gesture Smith and Carlos had at the ready and who had said, "I'll stand with you." It was Peter who, upon learning that Smith had only two black gloves for their post-race demonstration rather than the four they had planned on, suggested each of the two men wear and raise a single glove. They agreed. Smith's black glove went on his right hand, Carlos's on his left.

And it was Peter who, seeing a member of the US crew team walk by wearing an "Olympic Project for Human Rights" button, asked if he could use it and wear it on the medals podium.

If it doesn't seem like Peter's actions that day had the potential to be world-altering, well, let's put a magnifying glass back on the social and civil unrest around the globe back then—and in our era, too. In 1968, Black Americans were just a few years removed from having been told they could not eat at the same restaurant, drink from the same water fountain, or sit in the same section of a public bus as white people. Apartheid raged in South Africa. Aboriginal people in Australia suffered much the same racial indignation and had not been recognized as Australian citizens with full voting rights until 1962, two years before the United States Congress approved the Civil Rights Act. Six months before Smith, Peter, and Carlos stepped onto that Mexico City track, James Earl Ray murdered Martin Luther King Jr., tragically and prematurely ending the Atlanta preacher's promising civil rights career.

"*Perspective* is my big word," Matt said. "You have to put Peter's life in perspective." The stakes were different for Peter than they were for Smith and Carlos. The two African American sprinters had a cause to spotlight, and they were all in. Peter had a belief that the cause was just, and he joined the demonstration in his own way. But he must have instinctively known he would not be celebrated for it. As Matt said, "The world was dealing with massive racial issues—the assassinations of [Robert F.] Kennedy and MLK [Jr.], the treatment of aboriginals—for Peter to stand up as he did was remarkable to me."

More remarkable is that Peter's actions came fifty-plus years before the brutal murder of George Floyd by Minneapolis policemen, leaving many Americans wondering if race relations had really progressed at all. Similar questions have continued to reverberate in Australia to this day.

It makes me wonder, then, if there was some special sauce for Peter's simple-but-significant human-rights actions, on behalf of a cause he believed in—that childhood-instilled belief in treating people the same way regardless of their color or circumstances. Peter has shared that he was on the receiving end of negative comments and hate mail. So why had he stepped up, in a way that brought him no benefit and in fact had brought him grief?

Certainly, both Janita and Matt agreed that Peter's upbringing with Salvation Army values—"Salvos," they were called—had something to do with it. In *Salute*, Peter boiled his actions down to that early and lifelong belief in equal treatment for all. "It wasn't a matter of color; you liked someone because you liked him. I couldn't see why anyone would dislike or, to the nth degree, hate someone simply because they're a different color."

But beyond that, strands of caring and compassion just seemed to have been stitched into Peter's DNA. "What Peter did is just inherently Peter. I think it's as simple as that," said Janita, describing her father as a "kind and gentle" man. She relayed a story that had been shared by her "Nana" Thelma, who died in 2023 just a few days shy of her 102nd birthday. The story involved Peter bringing home and befriending boys of Japanese descent who had no other friends to speak of. "He became their best friend," Janita said. "I don't think it was the only time Peter did that."

At the same time, though, Janita thought back on the era in which Peter brought his human-rights beliefs to bear at great risk. It was not the usual set of actions for a Caucasian athlete, or any white man of the late 1960s, to take. "That's what makes it so incredible—it just wasn't done," she said. "He had to be incredibly courageous, and he did act out of his beliefs."

While Peter's post-race actions triggered some negative blowback, they didn't stain his standing with Athletics Australia officials—at least not in the immediate aftermath of the 200 meters. Strath Gordon, the chief of public affairs for the Australian Olympic Committee (AOC), passed along a story that was corroborated by Matt in our Zoom interview. The story was that an Athletics Australia team official, after warning Peter that some people might be out to get him, showed that the national team officials were not among them. The "punishment" the team doled out was to provide Peter with tickets to a hockey game that evening.

However, things got messy for Peter beginning with a series of events that took place after the 1968 Olympics. One bone of major

Members of Australia's track-and-field team had time for bonding before the 1968 Summer Games in Mexico City. Peter Norman is the second from the left and his fellow sprinter, Greg Lewis, is in the middle. Credit: Ray Weinberg

contention involved the 1972 Olympic Trials for Australian sprinters and the choice of who to take to the Summer Games in Munich. Athletics Australia, the nation's track-and-field body, had a qualifying standard of 20.9 seconds for the 200 meters. Peter had bested that plenty of times, but in the country's Olympic Trials in Perth, Peter—competing on an injured knee—took third place in 21.6 seconds. Lewis won the event, and a sprinter named Gary Eddy took second.

So, was that the sum of it? Did a thirty-year-old Peter simply fail to summon up a good enough performance at the very time he needed to? Did he doom himself by running a second slower than he had in Mexico City? Or had his post-race Mexico City actions somehow gotten in his way?

In our conversations, Gordon said Peter's failure to qualify for the 1972 Summer Games was not a reflection on his actions in Mexico City. "He was injured and at the end of his career when he failed to qualify for the next Games at the Olympic trials. He ran a poor time." In that same vein, a post–Olympic Trials article from *The Age*, a daily newspaper in Melbourne that has been published since 1854, quoted Peter as saying, "I'm history. I'm out of the team." The reporter, Ron

Carter, also wrote that Peter "probably ran himself out of the team at the National titles."

But there are more details to examine. In that same article in *The Age*, Carter noted that Peter had been nursing the aforementioned knee injury for weeks. "If the selectors do the right thing, Norman should still be on the plane to Munich. He has run 20.5 [seconds] this season and is a good competitor. In Munich, he would do well."

Then there was the confusion over what, if any, process existed on paper to guide Athletics Australia in its decision-making. In *The Peter Norman Story*, the authors quoted a national-team selector, Paul Jenes—the same man who referred to the 20.9-second standard—as saying, "There were no set criteria. You basically picked the best team."

If that was the case, Matt said, wouldn't it have made enormous sense to place Peter—Australia's national record holder, the 1968 silver medalist, and the world's fifth-ranked 200-meter runner—on the Australia team headed for Munich? "He qualified that year fifteen times for the 100 and 200," Matt said, adding that there had been other athletes taken based on previous achievements.

Whether Athletics Australia had latitude to use Peter's prior times and ranking to invite him, we will probably never know. "I'm not the historian to know the process the sport had," Gordon said. "It would have sat within the AOC's rules at the time." I couldn't access those rules, nor could the folks at the AOC.

What we do know is that nowadays, more than fifty years later, such rules are clearer and more finite—and, at least in the case of the United States, provide some flexibility for officials to go beyond just an Olympic Trials performance.

Gordon said, "These days, we have a very clear selection-policy process, which is agreed to with each team." The USATF's published rules indicated that "Athletes may meet the qualifying standard in one of two ways," either through the "qualifying standards as established by World Athletics" or "by virtue of his/her World Athletic Ranking Position for that event."

What made the whole saga of who Australia decided to send to Munich even odder and murkier is the curious fact that the country wound up not taking *any* male sprinters to Germany for the 1972 Olympic Games. We don't know what Peter would have done had he been in the field for Munich, but we do know that only one 200-meter sprinter in 1972, gold-medal winner Valeriy Borzov of the Soviet Union, ran a time faster than the one Peter recorded in Mexico City four years earlier.

More controversy crept up in 2000, when Australia hosted the Summer Olympics in Sydney, and questions arose as to whether Peter, a now-retired Olympic athlete, was accorded the respect he deserved as a former track-and-field luminary.

The way Gordon told it and the way IOC vice president and then AOC president John Coates described it in *The Peter Norman Story*, Peter indeed received his just due. He ran a leg of Australia's Olympic torch relay, served as an Australian Olympic Team ambassador at promotional events, and helped christen the Olympic medals that would be used for the 2000 Games during a gala at the famed Sydney Opera House.

But there were competing perspectives from the 2000 Summer Games, with Matt and others believing Peter was slighted. On the day Sydney kicked off the 2000 Summer Olympics, Peter was at Matt's wedding, where he was the emcee. Matt said, "He definitely was not invited to the opening ceremonies."

Both Coates and Gordon said that was because the opening ceremonies were a one-hundredth anniversary tribute to women being involved in the Olympic Games. Thus, after former one-mile world-record holder and 1960 Summer Games gold medalist Herb Elliott carried the Olympic flame into the stadium for those opening ceremonies, every other participant in the "lap of honour" was a female athlete: three-time silver-medal-winner Raelene Boyle, four-time Olympic champion Betty Cuthbert, four-time gold-medal-winner swimmer Dawn Fraser, and Cathy Freeman, who ran to 400-meter gold for her country in those 2000 Games. "The whole point was that we were celebrating the rich history of female athletes," said Gordon, who believed it was unjust to "reflect that Peter was treated unfairly. There was no resentment of Peter."

But Matt conveyed in our interview that while Peter *did* play a role in the lead-up to the 2000 Games in Sydney, Australian officials didn't invite him to any functions during the Games themselves. It seemed to be the United States, not Australia, that took extra steps to value Peter's presence and to finance his attendance at events during the Sydney Games. For example, a prominent USATF official, Steve Simmons, arranged airfare for Peter to travel from his home in Melbourne to Sydney, where he was warmly embraced and applauded as a guest of the US Olympic Committee (USOC). The USOC then flew Peter to a subsequent Olympic track-and-field Trials. Years later, retrospective articles on Peter indicated he had been "shunned" in 2000 and not invited to events.

Whether Peter was wrongly snubbed heading into Munich in 1972 or overlooked and underappreciated during the 2000 Summer Games—and whether any of that was an aftereffect of his 1968 stand for racial and human rights—will almost surely remain an unsettled debate. Clearly, there are different lenses to look through, just as there are different picture frames illustrating how Peter could be viewed.

Janita described her dad in one sense as "incredibly charismatic. You couldn't help but like him." But she also said her dad could be "fiery, outspoken, a pain in the ass, and a smart ass," and someone who at times "ruffled a few feathers and pissed people off."

Matt lovingly described his uncle's wonderful sense of humor, his skills as a magician, how he dressed up as Santa Claus during the holidays, and how Matt's wife fell in love with Peter because he was always "the kindest man in the room."

But Peter was not without his flaws and foibles. *The Peter Norman Story* is open and honest about Peter's struggles with alcohol, his bouts of depression, his cigarette-smoking addiction, his dependence on prescription painkillers following a devastating Achilles tendon injury in 1985, and his oft-strained relationship with his wives and kids.

Upon self-introspection, Peter seemed to understand that views of him ran the spectrum. Before the Olympic Trials controversy in 1972, he had complained bitterly about a whisker-close finish in the 100-meter finals at the 1972 Victorian State Championships, where he felt wronged by an Athletics Australia decision to award Lewis first place and him second. Peter told interviewers it may have been *that* controversy, as much as anything that happened on a medals stand with Smith and Carlos, that earned him the ire of Athletics Australia officials. "I earned the frowning eyes of the powers that be in track and field by misbehaving at the state championships when I honestly thought I had won the state 100-meter title. And the judges honestly thought I had run second."

Peter also described to those who chronicled him that there were three schools of thought on his actions in Mexico City: "There were those who approved of what I did, those who would have been happier if I hadn't done what I did, and those who said, 'You can count on Norman to do something stupid like that.'"

There are a diminishing number of Olympians alive to share their thoughts on Peter, but one who was alive and well as I wrote this book was his sprint rival Lewis, who settled in Melbourne for many years after a career in construction and running his own business. Lewis had several good perspectives to draw on about Peter and about track-and-field politics in Australia. One was that he ended his own sprinting career in disgust in 1976 after he was *not* named to the Australian Olympic Team heading to that year's Summer Games in Montreal while a sprinter whom Lewis had defeated in the Olympic Trials 200 meters was. A second was that Lewis's daughter, Tamsyn Manou, appeared in three Olympics as a runner and hurdler. And a third is the spirited rivalry he and Peter had.

While Lewis shared on one hand that he and Peter were fierce competitors who "never gave each other a millimeter" and that he felt Peter was "a master at being arrogant" at times, he also had retained fond memories of him, like drinking brandies at the bar after the Olympic sprint races were over. He also readily credited Peter with a "magnificent achievement" in 1968 for winning silver and running down Carlos. "Peter was eminently successful in 1968, and in some ways, that ended up being a drawback in his life." Looking back on the events of 1968, and his country's choice to not take Peter or any other sprinters to Munich in 1972, he said, "I'm quite convinced Peter was ostracized as a result. That's my view . . . He was virtually banned from the Olympic movement, either overtly or under cover."

At the same time, while Lewis pointed to Peter's Salvation Army beliefs and felt his Olympics teammate "was the model of propriety" on the medals podium in 1968, he believed Peter's crowning success story in Mexico City was his 200-meter sprint finish, not his human-rights stand. "He was no Joan of Arc [in Mexico City]," Lewis said, adding that Peter may have kept an eye on social issues but that his sprint rival "was certainly no crusading evangelist."

After not going to the 1972 Olympics and retiring from track and field, Peter had a professional career that went through a series of shifts and changes, from butcher to physical-education teacher to sports-and-recreation administrator and running coach. His side pursuits included theater performances, Australian rules football, fishing, and slot-car racing. In 2006, just months after he had undergone a triple bypass surgery to unblock his arteries, he died of a heart attack. He was only sixty-four years old.

But in the months before he died, Peter left a poignant reminder of the legacy Smith and Carlos carved out and that he had shared in. Peter had enjoyed a last reunion with Smith and Carlos—one of several that had occurred during the course of his life, as he, Smith, and Carlos segued from being partners in a human-rights demonstration to enjoying a warm and genuine friendship. A final reunion took place at San José State University, Smith and Carlos's alma mater, when university officials unveiled a statue of the two men to commemorate their ground-breaking efforts.

Peter was left out of the statue. But he responded with humility and grace versus outrage. "What was said to the world that day was there are a few things that aren't quite right. There's a few rules that don't quite add up. You can be who you are, you can do what you want, you can expect to get a lot of praise for that if you want . . . as long as your skin is white. You can be recognized for your achievements, you can stand tall anywhere you want and tell people what to do . . . as long as your skin is white . . . These two very dear friends of mine stood up and said, 'Oh no. You aren't going to bury me like that.'"

They were glowing words from a man who had his own shining human-rights moments on that day. But if Australia had been a little slow in recognizing the positive impact of what he did, perhaps Peter's funeral in 2006 turned the tide. Matt was intimately involved in the details and funding for that ceremony, which brought Smith and Carlos to the continent to speak and serve as pallbearers. Simmons, too, helped with the financial details and in arranging for USATF, in 2006, to mark October 9 as "Peter Norman Day," with a proclamation in honor of Peter's decision "to stand up for what was right, no

Janita Norman (left) reacts after the unveiling of a statue to honor her father, 1968 Olympic athlete Peter Norman, at Lakeside Stadium in Melbourne, Victoria, Australia on October 9, 2019. Credit: Michael Dodge / EPA-EFE / Shutterstock

matter the consequences." Simmons indicated to reporters that it was unprecedented for the USATF to declare a day in honor of an athlete outside of the United States.

At the funeral, both Carlos and Smith spoke eloquently of their competitor and colleague. Carlos: "Peter never flinched [on the dais]. He never turned his eyes, he never turned his head. He never said so much as 'ouch.' . . . Not every young white individual would have the gumption, the nerve, the backbone, to stand there . . . You guys have lost a great soldier . . . Go and tell your kids the story of Peter Norman." Smith: "He left a legacy for us to stand on. Stand on that rock, be proud. My friend, Peter Norman, the humanitarian who believed that right can never be wrong."

After Peter's death, Australian officials established additional tributes for him, as more and more Australians, and some Americans, developed a greater understanding of the magnitude of what the man did. A transformative one came on October 11, 2012, through the efforts of

Andrew Leigh, a member of Australia's Parliament. Leigh researched what had happened to Peter and believed an official mea culpa was in order. Leigh's motion of apology to Peter passed unanimously:

> *That this House: (1) recognises the extraordinary ath-*
> *letic achievements of the late Peter Norman, who won*
> *the silver medal in the 200-metres sprint running event*
> *at the 1968 Mexico City Olympics, in a time of 20.06*
> *seconds, which still stands as the Australian record; (2)*
> *acknowledges the bravery of Peter Norman in donning*
> *an Olympic Project for Human Rights badge on the*
> *podium, in solidarity with African-American athletes*
> *Tommie Smith and John Carlos, who gave the "black*
> *power" salute; (3) apologises to Peter Norman for the*
> *treatment he received upon his return to Australia, and*
> *the failure to fully recognise his inspirational role before*
> *his untimely death in 2006; and (4) belatedly recognises*
> *the powerful role that Peter Norman played in further-*
> *ing racial equality.*

In 2018, as part of the fiftieth-anniversary celebration of the Mexico City Olympics, the AOC awarded Peter with a posthumous Order of Merit, with the IOC's Coates acknowledging that the recognition and praise for Peter's stand should have come earlier.

Then, on October 9, 2019, Athletics Australia and the Victorian government unveiled a statue in Peter's honor in Melbourne's city center. Gordon of the AOC said that along with the statue, Athletics Australia established a Peter Norman Day to recognize his achievements. Peter's mother, Thelma, his daughter Janita, and his old coach, Neville Sillitoe, were there.

The AOC officials who organized that ceremony did not invite Matt to attend, which rankled him then and thereafter. "I was shunned for speaking Peter's truth," he said.

Gordon admitted that praise and recognition for what Peter did in 1968 "should have come much earlier." He added that "Australia, like the US, has needed to come to terms with our past and our history . . . Peter clearly said he believed in human rights. He took a stand."

I certainly agree with Gordon, with Peter's family, and with those who look back on the events in Mexico City. Very few white people were willing to stand up for the racial rights and equality of Black men and women in the late 1960s, and fewer still would have done it in such a public setting as an Olympic medals ceremony. Peter did both.

The irony is that with all the back-and-forth over his proper place in history, there's a fair chance Peter would have been a bit embarrassed by any hoopla. Matt described Peter as "the guy that stood back from the crowd," and he also said he took on the projects to shed light on Peter's life because his uncle never would have trumpeted those exploits on his own.

Further evidence of Peter's lack of hubris involves the silver medal he brought home from Mexico City. A lot of medals are paraded around prominently or placed in a centrally located trophy case for all to see. Not Peter's. His uncle, Matt joked, used *his* silver medal as a doorstop.

For her part, Janita has been hopeful that the focus on Peter would shift, moving the spotlight away from how he was treated and toward who he was and what he did for racial equality and human rights. She called her dad a "complex fella" but said that at the end of the day, the flashlight should shine on his actions. "Peter has been painted in a light of being a victim. I really want to change the narrative and look at the positive things Peter did. He did suffer poor treatment, and he went through a lot of challenges. But I hope that we can be using his story for positive change instead of seeing it as 'poor Peter.'"

Matt said he once had the opportunity to ask his uncle if, upon reflection, he would repeat his stand. Peter said, "Every single time." In *Salute*, Peter admitted he was "rather proud to be a part" of those Mexico City actions and felt lucky enough to be in the right places at the right times on many occasions. But at the end of that film, when asked how he wanted to be remembered, Peter fell back not on self-aggrandizing but on the modesty that also helped define his sixty-four-year run. "I guess I would just like to be thought of as an interesting old guy."

PART V

CREATING AND PRESERVING OLYMPIC VENUES

CHAPTER 12

SENAD OMANOVIĆ, BOSNIA AND HERZEGOVINA

1984 WINTER OLYMPICS, SARAJEVO

In 1984, the Sarajevo Olympics became the first Winter Games ever hosted by what had been a Communist country. They were hailed as a great success and a demonstration of global unity. Less than a decade later, bloodshed threatened to wash much of that goodwill away and collateral damage destroyed a key site from the Games.

While the trauma of human loss unfortunately remains, those who feared the Bosnian War would permanently paralyze Sarajevo's 1984 infrastructure have probably never met a determined former luger named Senad Omanović.

With his thick, gray hair, a bushy mustache, and a goatee, Senad, who was born in 1957, looked more like a college professor than a revolutionary on my Zoom screen. But don't let the kind eyes and mild manner fool you. Senad proved himself a spirited fighter who led a long battle to restore one of the 1984 Games's most acclaimed facilities, its luge and bobsled track, to its former glory.

"Most of my friends thought I was crazy and that this simply wouldn't be possible at all," wrote Senad, a three-time national champion in luge racing for his country. "They were rather skeptical." His brave and once-lonely undertaking to restore a beautiful facility eventually converted those skeptics while garnering attention and resources from key allies. But those old enough or steeped enough in history to understand what happened in 1992 could hardly be faulted for their apprehension. That was the year the fury of a three-year-long war resulted in the decimation of Sarajevo's Olympic Games facilities.

That war, known as the Bosnian War, started after full-scale fighting broke out in Croatia and after the breakup of what was then Yugoslavia. When the European Community, later designated the European Union, recognized Croatia's and Slovenia's independence late in 1991, it invited Bosnia and Herzegovina to apply for recognition as well. A referendum on independence then appeared on the ballot. Nearly all the two-thirds of the electorate who voted on that referendum chose an independent state. However, tensions then flared after independence had been proclaimed and after European Community negotiators promoted the division of Bosnia and Herzegovina into ethnic subdivisions.

Tensions turned into war on April 7, when Bosnian Serb paramilitary forces fired on Sarajevo and Bosnian Serb units of the Yugoslav army carried out artillery bombardments. Many Bosniaks (Bosnian Muslims) were subsequently expelled from cities such as Zvornik, Foča, and Višegrad by a combination of paramilitary forces and Yugoslav army units.

The war raged on until a 1995 ceasefire was negotiated by Western nations with the backing of the North Atlantic Treaty Organization (NATO). By then, 100,000 casualties had been left behind in the fighting among Bosniaks, Serbs, and Croats. Six years later, former Serbian president Slobodan Milošević was arrested and charged with genocide and war crimes against humanity. No city suffered more catastrophic damage than Sarajevo, the scenic mountain-and-river-framed capital city of Bosnia and Herzegovina (BiH). As many as 329 shellings a day rocked the city at the height of the war.

The center of the decimation had been Mount Trebević, ground zero for the luge and bobsled track events of the 1984 Winter Games.

As a result, virtually "all sports facilities were destroyed during the war," Senad wrote. Those who knew the majesty of the track firsthand must have found its devastation especially heart-wrenching. Built for those Games, with the German company of Die Deyle Gruppe Stuttgart doing planning and design and Sarajevo companies like Union Invest and GP Bosna working as subcontractors, the track was considered state of the art in several ways.

For one thing, the facility utilized sustainable materials and was engineered so it could be used by lugers and bobsledders during the Games and redesigned afterward for more recreational use, said Dr. Sanela Klarić, a professor of architecture at Sarajevo's International Burch University and a member of the federal parliament of Bosnia and Herzegovina. The designers also succeeded in developing a track that was "one of the few where both lugers and bobsledders liked it," said Svein Romstad, a transplanted Norwegian who was head coach of the US Luge Team in Sarajevo and who went on to a two-and-a-half-decade-long career as general secretary of the International Luge Federation (FIL). Romstad said that because lugers typically like tighter tracks while bobsledders value broader ones, building something equally well liked by both was quite a feat.

The coup de grâce, however, was a building component unique to the Sarajevo track. It was "a special feature that cannot be found on any other bobsled and luge track in the world," wrote Josef Fendt, who was the team leader for Germany's luge team at the 1984 Games and who served from 1994 to 2020 as president of the FIL. Specifically, Fendt wrote, the track had "hydraulically movable 'switches' [that] were built in two places to divide the track into three parts for training purposes."

Tragically, though, the track couldn't survive a barrage of mortar shells. It couldn't overcome the beating that came with Mount Trebević, in the present-day BiH capital city of Sarajevo, being used as an artillery base for military forces. It couldn't sidestep the damage that went with being an epicenter of years of deadly war.

In 1997, after the war had ended but with security forces still omnipresent, the FIL wanted firsthand insights into whether the venerable luge and bobsled track could be restored in some way. Because the track had been so heralded, it was important to the FIL to see if it could be rebuilt. But there wasn't a long line of volunteers who wanted to inspect the track and assess what needed to be done to fix it.

"No one signed up, so they said, 'Would you be willing to go?' And I said, 'Absolutely,'" said Bob Hughes. A member of the USA Luge board of directors who served as the 1984 USA Luge team's manager working alongside Romstad, Hughes became the longtime marketing director for USA Luge. Later, he cofounded Carr-Hughes, a highly successful television-production company for whom he served as executive producer for four Olympic Games.

The venture back to the luge and bobsled track tugged at Hughes's heartstrings for a couple of reasons. For one, he had helped Romstad take the US Luge Team to new heights in 1984, or as he joked: "We moved from being a comic relief act to 'OK, these guys know what side of the hill they're on.'" For another thing, Hughes was at the time in a relationship with a woman from Sarajevo.

When the time came to inspect the track, Hughes recalled being brought in by military escort. "We had to cross seventeen temporary bridges, and they're being guarded," he said. Hughes photographed and videotaped—and shared with Romstad—extensive footage and pictures of the devastation to the track, bullet holes and all. One of his particularly vivid memories was being in the upper parking lot where the men's bobsled starting gate was, "and it hits me: in the ground is where there is a [piece of a] bomb stuck." He saw "huge holes, eight-inches to a foot wide," and readily complied with directions from weapon-equipped peacekeepers who told the group not to touch anything that wasn't concrete.

Added Romstad: "I still have the pictures he sent me. It was horrific. Everything was stripped, with holes from the shooting—a horrible mess." Hughes said holes in the track also exposed and hastened the corrosion of refrigerated piping underneath the track, with the refrigeration ultimately transported back to Germany for safekeeping. Underground mines had to be removed and cleared as well.

Fendt wrote that, even when he and other FIL executive board members visited the facility in May 2015, after restoration work had finally begun, "You could still clearly see the shell holes from the war in the curves, which had been sealed with concrete again so that it was possible to slide on them with wheeled sleds."

The three-year-long Bosnian War decimated many of Sarajevo's 1984 Winter Games facilities, leaving visible bullet holes in the luge and bobsled track. Credit: Svein Romstad

The overall damage to the track was mind-numbing. And though there were conversations about doing something to rehabilitate it, Romstad and Hughes counted themselves among the initial doubters. "There was a lot of talk, but I never expected anything to come out of it," Romstad said. Yet, unknowingly, Hughes had stirred someone to action on his visit to the site on that day in 1997. There was a keen listener within the contingent when Hughes offhandedly suggested someone should take on the yeoman job of restoring the once glorious track.

"The idea was born in 1997, after the war and that visit from Bob Hughes," said Sabina Omanović, the eldest of Senad's three daughters and the translator for our Zoom interview. Unfortunately, while the *idea* may have been hatched in 1997, it would take many years for a sparsely financed, all-volunteer effort to grow into something more substantial. Senad had begun to invest some of his own money at the outset but indicated he stopped doing so after initial promises of help failed to materialize. It wasn't until 2014 that significant cleanup of the track finally began in earnest. Still, learning of the initiative that the 1997 visit had spawned and the role Senad assumed in trying to make the longshot project a reality, Hughes said, "I was surprised—pleasantly surprised."

One of the most pleasant surprises for the FIL and the people of Sarajevo was Senad's determination to make a difference. When he took on the luge-and-bobsled reclamation endeavor, the FIL gained a leader who had already invested the better part of his life in the sport of luge—six years as a competitor and thirty-three more as a coach, including two years coaching the Yugoslavian national team and many more with the Bosnia and Herzegovina national team after 1993. Plus he had national team experience with Croatia and Serbia prior to that. With Senad, the officials had a true patriot, too—a man who stayed in BiH to serve as a member of Bosnia's special police force during the war, even as his wife, Izeta, and their three young daughters fled to Switzerland in 1993 for safety. Senad's family returned in 1997.

Senad blended devotion to his sport and patriotism to his country with a devout enthusiasm for the rebuilding task at hand. He thought it would be a shame if the track could not be restored as a place for training, recreation, and perhaps someday, competitions. "Our track is one of the most beautiful but also one of the fastest and technically hardest," he said through Sabina. "This was also one of the most secure tracks. There were no severe injuries [sustained] on it."

But bringing a debilitated track back to health was a slow and arduous process. To begin with, there were trees growing out of the track, not to mention graffiti and trash galore. Job one for Senad and other volunteers was using their own money and tools to complete a massive cleanup mission, which included fixing bullet holes and removing underground hazards.

More help came from the FIL, which had been interested in rehabilitation from day one and became impressed with the work Senad and others were doing. The FIL provided what Fendt described as "start-up aid"—fifteen sleds, a transport vehicle, and a variety of equipment such as helmets and racing shoes, worth what he estimated to be about €30,000, or a little over $33,000 in US money at the time.

"Senad was the 'motor' of the team of volunteers in BiH with the aim of using the track for luge again. He also established important contacts with a school in Sarajevo to get young athletes there interested in luge," Fendt wrote. "Senad was very enthusiastic and passionate about this cause, for which I admired him."

One of the most important contacts Senad made was Dr. Klarić, a political and academic force who has emerged as a critical yin to his yang in the track-restoration effort. Her help was vital as she sought

Parliament's help with an action plan to ultimately restore not only the bobsled and luge track but the 1984 Games ski-jumping and biathlon facilities as well. With her Burch University hat on, she also worked with architects and students writing their master's thesis on the track-restoration project. A quiet but steady momentum began building.

Dr. Klarić first met Senad in 2016 after she talked with Burch University's office of urban planning about the luge and bobsled track project, and they suggested she reach out to him. It became a potent partnership, one where "I found the strength in him, and he found the strength in me," Dr. Klarić said.

What was possible to begin with was a "walk before you can run" approach. The FIL, Senad, Dr. Klarić, and others reasoned that it was economically viable to use the existing track, to clear it enough to accommodate equipment on wheels, and to feature it as a summer training track, in large part because there are only a handful of sanctioned training facilities in all of Europe.

Within a year, what had once been an iced-down 1,300-meter bobsled track and 1,210-meter luge track transformed into a facility where wheeled equipment could zoom downhill at high speeds. What was once modestly seen as a place to create summer training opportunities for BiH racers became an international training ground. And the graffiti ended up being a tourist draw of sorts. Other parts of the world took notice of a reinvigorated track roaring back to relevance.

"Sarajevo Olympic bobsled, luge track restored, in use again after Bosnian war," proclaimed a headline from an October 31, 2016, NBC Sports article. "Bosnia's war-ravaged Olympic track comes back to life," chimed in the BBC, in a headline to a September 22, 2017, article. Sabina said junior and senior athletes from Poland, Slovakia, Slovenia, and Turkey, among others, came to use the Sarajevo track for summer training.

However, another challenge came forth—one Senad, Dr. Klarić, and their growing band of helpers could not have foreseen. In March 2020, the COVID-19 pandemic struck with a vengeance, halting the forward movement for a few years, though not stopping it altogether.

Beyond COVID, Senad and Sabina said there were other hurdles to clear. One involved the sad fact that, for reasons that can't be easily explained, the luge and bobsled track was never recognized or legalized

Years before real resources materialized for the cleanup of the Olympic Games luge and bobsled track, Senad Omanović led a volunteer effort to restore it. Credit: Senad Omanović

as a formal property. Senad indicated that the company that owns the Olympic facilities never registered the facility, and Sabina said work to designate the track as a legal property began around 2019. Once that is accomplished, a value can be put on it and future investors can be tapped.

There have also been never-ending scrambles to round up scant funding and to convince the political powers that the rebuild of the luge and bobsled track deserves their attention.

"It is true, we need to have a lot of patience," Dr. Klarić said, "but we can now say we have all the stakeholders on board. It will take time because there are so many other priorities [for BiH]." Those other priorities include everything from governance reform and revamping of election laws to contemplating membership in the European Union and NATO. Still, Dr. Klarić said, "We believe this is something that really needs to be protected and used."

In the category of making progress, Dr. Klarić said she and Senad have been able to add the mayor of Sarajevo as an ally as well as a work group formed in partnership with the new minister of culture and sports for Sarajevo Canton, a territorial district that includes nine municipalities. In fact, the new minister is a former bobsled competitor who backs their efforts, Dr. Klarić said. They have also worked to form more alliances and coalitions for the long haul.

In the meantime, Sarajevo brings considerable attributes and assets to the table to boost the efforts to rebuild the track. The scenic beauty of the city is a draw for tourists, as is the artwork on the luge and bobsled track, which has made it a unique magnet for hikers and bikers alike. Also, a cable car in Sarajevo's city center can whisk visitors up to the top of Mount Trebević within ten minutes, where they are treated to a spectacular view of the municipality below them and a scenic mountaintop with flora, greenery, and quaint cafes.

"Sarajevo is pretty connected with the rest of Europe and the world," Sabina said, noting that roads, trains, and an airport make the city exceptionally easy to access. Additionally, the Adriatic Sea is only a little over two hundred kilometers—a two-hour drive—away.

Senad and Dr. Klarić also had hoped that the year 2024, as the fortieth anniversary of the 1984 Winter Games, would lend an added boost to their efforts. They hoped to draw on the success those games enjoyed, particularly in contrast to some of the turbulence of prior Olympic Games: the 1972 Summer Games in Munich marred by tragedy with terrorists invading the Olympic Village and killing two Israeli National Team members while taking nine others hostage and ultimately killing them as well; scores of nations boycotting the 1980 Summer Olympics in Moscow in protest of Russia's invasion of Afghanistan; and four years later, Russia's boycott of the 1984 Summer Games in Los Angeles as part of a fourteen-nation bloc of Eastern European countries.

By comparison, the Sarajevo Games celebrated a worldwide contingent of 1,272 athletes from forty-nine countries coming together and competing for glory. Host Yugoslavia won its first-ever Winter Olympic medal that year, a silver in giant slalom for alpine skier Jure Franko. The United States took home four gold and four silver medals, including its first-ever gold medal in downhill skiing. Official reports indicated that the 1984 Winter Games turned a profit of ten million dollars, which is all but unheard of these days.

Beyond the numbers, there will be fond memories for all those involved in and rooting for the restoration of Sarajevo's luge and bobsled track.

Fendt remembered leading the German luge team into the capital of BiH. "I remember that the Olympic Games were well-organized, and we had a beautiful view of the city of Sarajevo from our sports facility on Mount Trebević," he noted. "Of course, I especially remember that we were able to win a gold medal with our luge team in doubles."

Romstad and Hughes recalled the 1984 Games as a turning point for USA Luge. In the years leading up to the Games, Hughes said, "I was looking for a coach, and it's a hundred dollars a week, and you have to pay your own room and board."

In 1984, though, the luge doubles team of Doug Bateman and Ron Rossi finished ninth, helping USA Luge crack the top ten for the first time ever. Additionally, Frank Masley finished fourteenth in luge singles and thirteenth in doubles and was selected as the Team USA flag carrier for the opening ceremonies, which "helped put US Luge on the map," Romstad said.

And Senad? He did not compete or coach in the 1984 Games, but the year will always be very special for him: it was when Sabina was born.

Dr. Klarić, who remembered attending events at those 1984 Games, looked at the fortieth-anniversary celebration as a way to honor the German company that worked on the luge and bobsled track and, importantly, to galvanize more support and funding. She said a series of February 2024 events, two of which she hosted, came off without a hitch, bringing renewed attention to Sarajevo's place as an Olympic site and fueling the city's hopes that it can successfully bid on the 2032 Winter Youth Olympic Games.

It will ultimately take tens of millions of dollars to *fully* restore the luge and bobsled track as a winter-worthy facility, and Senad's dream of accomplishing that ultimate goal has remained strong. Dr. Klarić has been astonished at how much Senad has worked to keep the fire burning for their project. "He's really strong, and I'm really amazed with his energy," she said. "It is an amazing job he did without any strategic support, and when he could not count on any government support."

Romstad echoed those sentiments regarding Senad, whom he called "incredibly passionate." He said of Senad and other volunteers, "It's been very heartwarming to see. They busted their butts, and knowing what they went through with the war, it is remarkable."

All that said, Senad and Sabina would be the first to stress that their endeavor has been a team effort. They applauded Dr. Klarić for her assistance. They pointed to Miralem Cirkinagic, the father of one of Senad's luge athletes, as another key supporter. They noted that the athletes themselves took on numerous volunteer tasks. And they saluted Senad's wife of over forty years. "My mom is his biggest supporter," Sabina said. "Even as he was going to give up, she helped him keep it going."

Someday, the Omanovićs hope they can look back and see their restoration project—the seed they planted decades ago—come into full bloom.

"It's been a hard journey for [Senad], for all his athletes, and for the family," Sabina said. But at the end of the day, for her father, "it is very important that the track lives on and that, in the future, it will be fully recovered and will serve as an international meeting point for all the athletes."

CHAPTER 13

ALEXANDER CUSHING, USA

1960 WINTER OLYMPICS, SQUAW VALLEY (NOW PALISADES TAHOE)

Imagine, some seventy years ago, promoters beginning the campaign to recruit the 1960 Winter Olympics to Squaw Valley and snowplowing headlong into a barrage of bemused expressions, raised eyebrows, rolled eyeballs, snickers and jeers, and patronizing pats on the head.

There were good reasons for the mountains of skepticism that greeted Alexander "Alex" Cushing, a transplanted New Yorker, as he and others sought to do the improbable. Back then, the Winter Olympics had never been held in the western half of either the United States or North America.

Back then, few people had ever heard of Squaw Valley. It was merely an unincorporated area, absent a defined community, a mayor, and political clout.

Back then, the full-service ski "resort" at Squaw Valley consisted of little more than a double chair lift, two rope tows, and a base lodge that ended up being reconstructed after a fire.

Cities in Europe, especially those clustered near and amid the Alps, viewed hosting the Winter Olympic Games as their preordained right. With the one exception of a 1932 outlier when Lake Placid claimed the Games, it *had* been. So the initiative to bring the Games to California was belittled as a stunt and dismissed as a marketing ploy, even— perhaps cunningly so—by Alex himself.

Despite those formidable obstacles, a funny thing happened on the way to a supposed surefire failure: Alex and his inner circle won the day. And, in the process, they launched an Olympics that was both successful and transformational, with the 1960 Games changing many things: the way the world views North Lake Tahoe and the mountains surrounding it, the images we conjure of Olympic opening ceremonies, the choreography of the Games that play out on our television sets, and even the instant-replay feature we now take for granted as we watch sporting events from the comforts of a living-room couch. Heck, they even gave us the *forgotten* "Miracle on Ice," two decades before the 1980 version came along.

Some of the main characters involved in the buildup of Squaw Valley, or the yeoman's work to bring the 1960 Winter Games there— notably Alex and a major landowner named Wayne Poulsen—are long gone by now. But many remain, including members of the Cushing and Poulsen families, an Olympian, volunteers who helped make the Games happen, those who wrote books about the underdogs, and producers of a documentary on the Hail Mary pass that led to an Olympic Games touchdown.

To pinpoint the driving force behind the pitch for Squaw Valley, we need look no further than Alex, who died in 2006 at age ninety-two. His onetime legal adviser and third wife, Nancy Cushing Evans, called her husband of nineteen years "larger than life" and "extremely resourceful." She also said he was "dangerously persuasive."

"Alex was actually a shy person," Nancy said, "but once he started talking, he could go on and on and mesmerize you. He just had that quality that few people have." She added that he had a dream, "and when he saw Squaw Valley, he was awestruck. He viewed the mountain as a sculpture."

"He was a visionary, no question about that," said award-winning author David Antonucci, who wrote a 2009 book about the 1960 Games aptly titled *Snowball's Chance.* Asked whether anyone besides

Alex could have made the longshot bid happen, Antonucci said, "It's doubtful . . . He knew how to get things done."

There were a few concentric circles that combined to help Alex get things done when it came to snaring the prize of the Winter Olympics. Surely, one of them was an inner drive he formed at an early age. Another was a competitive fire that burned in him—and that had its flames fanned when other US cities maneuvered to put their names in the hat for the 1960 Games. But before the inner drive and the competitive juices could flow, Alex had to grow to love the beauty, majesty, and awesome potential of a virtually untapped mountain range surrounding the Central Valley of California and spilling into parts of Nevada. That all took root in 1946 when he visited Squaw Valley with friends.

One of the friends Alex traveled with, Alexander McFadden—who would later tragically die in an avalanche in Aspen, Colorado—had had a chance encounter with Wayne, and he brought Alex and Wayne together to scout out the mountain. Through those early visits, Alex formed a passion and a vision for what Squaw Valley could become.

But well before 1946, Wayne already had established his own mind's-eye view of the area, believing that it could and should accommodate a world-class destination ski resort. "He understood the value of Squaw Valley immediately upon seeing it," said Russell Poulsen, the youngest of Wayne and Sandy Poulsen's eight kids.

Interestingly, Alex and Wayne were polar opposites in many ways. Alex was a novice skier, while Wayne was a champion ski jumper and skier who would be inducted into the US Ski and Snowboard Hall of Fame in 1980. Alex was a New York and Wall Street–trained lawyer who brought East Coast instincts to the West Coast; Wayne was a westerner through and through and had been a Boy Scout and an Eagle Scout as a youngster growing up in Reno. Like Wayne had before, Alex saw the possibilities for harnessing the land on which Squaw Valley sat, but he didn't own any of it.

Russell said that it was 1943 when his dad purchased the first 640 acres of what would become the Squaw Valley Resort. His parents then grew their acreage to 2,000, as the prior landowner, the Southern Pacific Railroad, sold off land it viewed at the time as being of minimal value. Yet Wayne cherished that land and saw firsthand the need to unlock it, his son explained.

"My father was a lover of skiing who enjoyed the mountains. Initially as a teen, he would compete whenever he could . . . but at that time, the roads in the Sierra Nevada closed in the wintertime, and the only path through was by train."

On the path to transform Squaw Valley, Wayne and Alex became partners who, at least initially, had complementary roles. Wayne owned the land for the Squaw Valley Development Company, and Alex took on the job of building a ski resort and raising the significant funds required to do so. Although that partnership would eventually take a sour turn, it relied in its early days in part on the enormous reservoir of mental fortitude that Alex called upon to tackle the task of developing a ski resort and competing for an Olympic Games.

While the idea of a world-class ski resort was a goal shared by both Alex and Wayne, the notion of bringing the Olympic Games to the Sierra Nevadas was Alex's brainchild. Nancy said her late husband's upbringing helped prepare him for the audaciousness of that initiative. "We're talking about someone sent away to boarding school when he was seven years old and put on a train from New York to Aiken, South Carolina, by himself," she shared. "His mother said, 'You'll have to make your own way.' He learned early to be tough and resilient."

Nancy explained how her husband had other life experience in surmounting challenges, such as when he went to the US Supreme Court to argue a case as a young attorney with the Justice Department. Or when, later, as a Naval logistics officer stationed in Brazil, he successfully lobbied Congress for a change in law after learning of prohibitions that precluded officials from sending war supplies from one location to another. Those nonstop lobbying efforts, which kept him up for six straight days, were a contributing factor to the Bell's palsy Alex contracted, Nancy said, leading to the paralysis of his facial nerves and weakness in the muscles on one side of the face.

Thus, it was a battle-tested Alex who had to absorb one setback after another en route to constructing a ski resort at Squaw Valley. In the initial years of the operation, Alex dealt with multiple avalanches that knocked out the only ski lift and a severe flood that wrecked

the only bridge. Then, after fighting back repeatedly against Mother
Nature, he geared up for a skirmish in 1954 when he learned from
newspaper accounts that officials in places like Reno and Anchorage
fancied *their* communities as suitable hosts for the 1960 Winter
Games. That was when Alex began spinning the wheels for his own
Olympic Winter Games recruiting job.

"He was somewhat incensed, as he knew that he had a much better
mountain," said Alexandra Howard, the youngest of three daughters
Alex had with his first wife, Justine Cutting Cushing.

As he prepared for the against-all-odds effort to bring a worldwide
sporting phenomenon to the North Lake Tahoe area, Alex made it a
point to manage expectations, perhaps his own included. Even though
his ego and his surroundings helped feed serious—albeit longshot—
ambitions of competing for an Olympic Games, he downplayed the
effort as little more than a marketing ploy and a publicity stunt, famously telling *Time* magazine in 1959 that he "had no more interest in
getting the Games than the man in the moon."

Those who knew Alex intimately wondered if those public comments and the downplaying of his chances tucked neatly into a
highly strategic effort to simmer down the pressure and give himself
breathing room to take on a mission he fully intended to complete.
Nancy called the statements "a sardonic moment" and indicated, like
Alexandra did, that the early lineup of competing venues in states such
as Alaska and Nevada lit a fire under Alex. Referring to the Alyeska
Resort near Anchorage, which Alex saw as the competition, Nancy
said he figured "if Alyeska can get the Games, then he could certainly
get the Games."

Alexandra said her dad saw in Squaw Valley a virtually untouched
beauty and an incomparable physical setting to build an Olympic
Stadium and Olympic Village from scratch. "I think the reason my
father was so effective in infusing the US Olympic Committee, and
then the International Olympic Committee, with the confidence that
Squaw Valley could host the Olympic Games was that he believed in
what he was saying."

While Alex and others faced difficult terrain, they also brought a
series of strengths to bear. Many of those emanated from Alex himself:
the force of his personality, his gifts for persuasion and negotiation,

Alex Cushing with his third wife, Nancy Cushing Evans, in 1995. As legal counsel and CEO of Squaw Valley Ski Corporation, Nancy played a key role in building up Palisades Tahoe to the world-class resort it is today. Credit: Alexandra C. Howard Collection

his aversion to the word *no*, his steel will, and the extent to which he was plugged in politically. "He was an easterner and well-to-do—and all the things that represents. But you had to admire the way he went about it," said Eddy Ancinas, a lifelong resident of the area who met her husband, two-time Alpine skiing Olympian Osvaldo Ancinas, at those 1960 Games. She was also an award-winning author who covered the history of Squaw Valley, in part, in her book *Squaw Valley & Alpine Meadows: Tales from Two Valleys*. "With Alex on board, you had the money and the connections."

Alongside Alex's personal attributes, Lake Tahoe and the Sierra Nevadas brought a bevy of natural ones. While the area was not yet ground zero for skiing aficionados, it did have the Sugar Bowl ski area at nearby Donner Summit, and it had been enough of a winter destination for Lake Tahoe to submit a letter of interest for the 1932 Winter Olympics. The area also boasted a climate that combined 250 or more sunny days a year with annual snowfall averaging more than 400 inches a year.

Both Antonucci and Russell emphasized another global force that played into Squaw Valley's favor when it emerged as a serious candidate. It was the mid-1950s, only a decade removed from the closing chapters of World War II, which saw the United States take on the massive effort of defending the leading nations of Western Europe and then expending vast sums to rebuild those war-torn countries.

"The European nations got back on their feet by the grace of the American people and the Marshall Plan pulling them out of the brink of disaster," said Russell. "There was an enormous amount of gratitude after World War II." Antonucci questioned how the Europeans could possibly have said no to the United States for the Olympic Games after the high cost incurred in helping liberate them from the Nazis. "I never saw that argument, but it had to be in the minds of the people sitting there [to vote]."

But European gratitude for the war efforts went only so far. Nancy said the European nations had predetermined they were going to vote for a location in Austria, so Alex still needed more fundamental assistance—support, money, and momentum. He got the first two rolling by energizing a *San Francisco Examiner* sports editor named Curley Grieve to endorse the 1960 bid and by capitalizing on his relationship with then California governor Goodwin Knight. Alex persuaded Knight to cast his support and request funding from the state to back the initiative. He also received financial assistance from well-known businessman and philanthropist Laurance Rockefeller.

Momentum swung further in Alex's direction when he persuaded a Harvard University classmate, George Weller, to help market and publicize the bid for the 1960 Games. Weller, a journalist for both the *New York Times* and the *Chicago Daily News* and a 1943 Pulitzer Prize recipient, lent significant credibility to the Squaw Valley bid.

One more Harvard classmate, ex–US State Department official Marshall Hazeltine, would be prescient in tag-teaming with Weller to court IOC voters. Historical reports of the lead-up to the votes for the 1960 Games indicated that Weller wooed delegates by speaking five languages, while Hazeltine fluently spoke three.

In addition, World War II hero Jo Marillac came on board. After his heroic and daring work in support of the French resistance, he moved to the United States and in 1951 accepted an offer to be an instructor at the nascent ski school at Squaw Valley when the "resort" consisted of only a single chairlift. Later, Marillac—a highly acclaimed mountaineer who eventually became the director of Squaw Valley's ski school—accompanied Alex to Paris to lobby the IOC and to help convince its officials that sun-drenched California also had mountains with prodigious snowfall. That was a big deal, because the prevailing mental image of California, even in that pre–Beach Boys era, was that of a state characterized by sun and surf, not skis and snow.

Alexandra, who took her first skiing lessons from Marillac, said that his "simply being head of the ski school would have been a validation of Squaw Valley to the French." Ancinas said bringing Marillac into the fold "was Cushing's first unconscious but brilliant step."

When it came time for the French and other members of the IOC to gather in Paris and cast their votes on a venue for the 1960 Games, the results were mind-blowing. There were actually three votes—a first where no site received a clear majority, followed by a secret evening vote where Squaw Valley and Innsbruck tied at thirty-one votes apiece, and a third and final vote where the upstarts from California prevailed by the narrowest of margins, 32–30.

Antonucci and Ancinas agreed that the result startled both Alex and the Austrian delegation, and it also befuddled longtime IOC president Avery Brundage, who scoffed that Cushing and the Squaw Valley delegation would "set back the Olympic movement twenty-five years." Ancinas's book colorfully captures the reaction Brundage had when Alex asked him how *he* would have voted, with the IOC president sharing that he would have "jumped out the window."

Even after that 1955 vote on where to hold the 1960 Games, the Squaw Valley promoters still had to secure funding from the state of California to make what was a provisional award an official one. Once said funding was in place, Brundage, in April 1956, officially declared the 1960 Winter Games had been awarded to Squaw Valley. Alex and company had seemingly done the impossible.

In our interview, Nancy said one thing that helped make the impossible possible was Alex's ability to sell the IOC on the premise that the Winter Olympics belonged to the whole world, not just to countries on one continent. Until then, Winter Olympic venues had been overwhelmingly clustered near the Alps, making the Winter Games the near-exclusive domain of the Europeans.

Nancy also referred to Alex's uncanny ability to take assumed negatives and turn them into positives. "As he said, 'If you have a lemon, make lemonade.'" To take that analogy and run with it, you could say there were at least two sour lemons that produced sweet lemonade for Alex: the oversize model he had commissioned to demonstrate what a Squaw Valley Olympic Village would look like and the compact layout of the Olympic Village.

The model built to show IOC officials was so heavy that it had to be shipped over to Paris on a special cargo plane. Then, it was too large to fit into the convention-center space the IOC had rented for its deliberations and its final voting. So, Alex and Hazeltine arranged to have the model displayed at the US Embassy in Paris.

Suddenly, Alex's challenge became a golden opportunity and a strategic decision. "He walked each of the committee members to the American Embassy—a ten-minute walk over and back," Nancy said. "He had this one-on-one time with committee members. No one had ever met with each of them." Alexandra echoed this point, indicating that her dad and Hazeltine made great use of these strolls, where they "had a delegate's undivided attention."

As for the layout of the Olympic Village, the intimacy of the facilities would become one of the 1960 Games's greatest assets. Before then, Olympic venues typically separated athletes from one another, putting each national team in its own hotel facilities. But at Squaw Valley, the Olympic Village housing for the athletes was built immediately adjacent to nearly all the event facilities. This departure from the tradition of lodging them off-site may have seemed to outsiders to be a big disadvantage but ended up being a major positive.

Both Antonucci and Ancinas said that the fact that the skating events, Alpine skiing events, and the 80-meter ski jump were within walking distance of one another—and of the Village where the athletes stayed—created unprecedented convenience, intimacy, and viewing for athletes and spectators alike. Four years later, when the Olympics were held in Innsbruck, Osvaldo Ancinas and other athletes "were all talking about how it [Squaw Valley] was the last Olympics created for the athletes." Antonucci added, "It was a small, intimate venue where the public could interact with athletes as they went back and forth and where the parking was close by." He called it "the last of the small, intimate Olympics, which is what Cushing had proposed to the IOC."

In retrospect, Alex had done so many things so well in the lead-up to the Games, in the lobbying for Squaw Valley and in creating a setting that was second to none, that it made abundant sense to sound the applause for what he and his team pulled off. Alex would later be inducted into the US Ski and Snowboard Hall of Fame in 2003 and remembered as a "founding father" and hero of Squaw Valley. In a 2006 obituary, the *Sierra Sun* newspaper hailed Alex as the man who "brought worldwide attention to the Tahoe ski resort."

But rewinding back to the 1950s, 1960, and the years afterward is an exercise that demonstrates an Alex revered by some and vilified by others. There is no question that Alex was about barreling toward a final destination, about going through some and over the heads of others, and about taking on governmental entities that stood in his way.

"He had a history of forging ahead, doing things and getting things done amid controversy—a 'just do it and ask for forgiveness' later approach," Antonucci said. In that same vein, Larry Sevison, who lived his entire life in the area, remembered plenty of tussles with Alex. Sevison served as a volunteer driver for the 1960 Games and later went on to a long career in county government and a post as an elected member of the Placer County Board of Supervisors.

"Alex was often ragging on me for one thing or another. He could be madder than a hatter one day, and the next day we were close friends and he wanted to have me for dinner . . . Alex wanted people around him that could help him." Sevison, however, also said Alex's behavior and approach evolved over time. "I think he ultimately got over what I would call his eliteness, and we had an ongoing relationship."

At the end of the day, Antonucci and Sevison said Alex should be accorded due credit. "People were slow to understand what he was doing," Sevison said, "but they're still enjoying it today."

In Alex's defense, too—as Nancy, Ancinas, and Russell underscored—he literally and figuratively had to move mountains, battling with a wide array of local, state, and federal agencies to get Squaw Valley built. The support for his efforts could be grudging at times. To cite one example, the Placer County Board of Supervisors went on record on March 11, 1958, in official support of hosting the 1960 Olympics to assist with efforts to secure state funding. However, their resolution cast the Olympic Games as a spectacle that would cause difficulties and burden taxpayers:

> *WHEREAS, there will be several thousands of people working in and around the area in construction business activities . . . and, WHEREAS, many of these people will create tremendous problems which will have to be borne by the taxpayers of Placer County.*

Ancinas, who for many years ran a ski shop with her husband and got to know Alex socially, said building a ski resort in those days almost *required* a bull-in-a-china-shop mentality. "To get a ski area, that is what you had to do," she explained. Nancy said her husband had to negotiate with the US Army Corps of Engineers, the US Forest Service, the railroad, the state of California, local officials, and more. Russell added that his dad "came to have a lot of respect for Alex Cushing and his ability to accomplish things. California is an almost impossible place to get things done."

While Alex fought to get things done *for* Squaw Valley, Wayne waged a vital war of his own to keep things from being done *to* Squaw Valley. In preparation for the Olympics, the state and the Corps had a plan to put in what Russell called "a massive parking lot" to serve the needs of the IOC. Wayne's heroic role was to fight with all his being against the state. "They wanted a parking lot twice the size," Russell said. "It would have covered the meadow halfway down." As it was, he said, a large parking area was still constructed, but Olympic officials were persuaded to use compacted snow and ice and wood chips that would eventually allow the meadow to recover. It preserved much more of the area that people revel in today when they ski Palisades Tahoe.

Wayne was "very proud of the end result, to preserve much of the valley," his son said, but the whole episode left permanent psychological scars on him. "He was demonized by the state of California and the press at the time," and a perception spread that his dad was anti-Olympics, which couldn't have been further from the truth. "My father was a delegate for the US Ski team and attended [practically] every Winter Olympics Games there had ever been."

And then there was the falling out between Alex and Wayne. The partnership they began when they toured the mountain and grew excited over what it would become ended up eroding and dissolving completely. Wayne, who frequently had to be away from the area in his work as a pilot for now-defunct Pan American Airlines, came home one day to learn that he had been forced out and that Alex had been named president of the Squaw Valley Development Company. Although Wayne would retain control of much of the land within Squaw Valley, Alex took over the job of building the lifts, the lodge, and the ski resort beginning the summer before the ski area's opening in 1949.

Retracing the steps of exactly who did what to whom in this come-apart between two proud and successful businessmen is, in part, a matter of perspective. Both Alexandra and Nancy described it as a difference of opinion over how the Squaw Valley area should be developed, and Russell agreed to some extent, referring to "a fundamental difference philosophically" in terms of what was the best way to go about developing the area and creating an internationally known skiing destination. Whatever led to the fissure between Alex and Wayne, some on the outside built it into a "Hatfield-McCoy Feud" of sorts. A perception within the community that the two men and the two families didn't want anything to do with one another was reinforced by Placer County Board of Supervisors member Cindy Gustafson. In the late 1980s and early 1990s, when Gustafson worked as a marketing and events manager for the Resort at Squaw Creek, she said if the Cushings and Poulsens were both going to be at an event, "my job was to have them be at opposite ends of the dance floor."

In reality, the relationship was more complex than that. Nancy called some of the external assumptions "way overbaked" and said reporters delighted in playing up the idea of feuding former partners. "A lot of journalists loved to emphasize the split. It made for good reading." Both Russell and Alexandra noted as well that the children of both families grew up with one another and often spent time together. It all added up to a lifelong relationship that is not easily pigeonholed. Russell said that when he would talk to his dad years later about Alex, his own father seemed to be of mixed minds.

After Squaw Valley's successful bid on the 1960 Winter Olympic Games, Alex Cushing (far left) poses in front of a poster with (from left) State Senator Biz Johnson and Wayne and Sandy Poulsen. Credit: Alexandra C. Howard Collection

On the one hand was a part of his dad that "never liked the man and couldn't stand his company." On the other, his father readily credited Alex with playing an integral part in building what became one of the world's top skiing havens. "Alex had made him a wealthy man . . . I think in his mind, the state of California was a bigger demon than Alex ever was."

When it came to the Olympic Games themselves, Alex himself may have been of mixed minds, too. The Olympic Organizing Committee established by the IOC decided there was a conflict of interest for Alex to be directly involved in the planning of the 1960 Winter Olympics, the idea being that the person with financial interest in the ski resort would find it challenging to stay unbiased in the planning efforts for the Games. It was a slight that led Alex to complain to *Time* magazine that he had been treated "like a criminal," according to a *New York Times* obituary published August 22, 2006.

But complaints around the Games and reservations as to whether

Squaw Valley was a suitable site have melted away for the most part, washed aside by an eleven-day-long Olympics that was nothing short of magnificent. For the Games that took place from February 6 to the 18, the North Lake Tahoe area welcomed some thirty countries and six hundred and sixty-five athletes competing in twenty-seven different events.

To put on such a production required not only the presence of officials paid to stage the games but also a massive volunteer turnout. Sevison was among the hordes of helpers who took on a myriad of tasks, including driving dignitaries from around the world who were seeing this foreign land for the first time. Sevison's passengers included well-known radio and television personality Art Linkletter, but his favorite story involved eight or nine members of Japan's hockey team, who crammed into his vehicle for the drive from the airport in Reno to the Olympic Village.

"We ran into bumper-to-bumper traffic, and they all jumped out of the car and were running alongside it, going up to other cars and trading [Olympic] pins with anybody and everybody." He called his assignment "one of those crazy experiences you have for a lifetime."

The crazy experiences extended to the weather, too, which was foreboding and mercilessly dispensing rain, sleet, hundred-mile-an-hour wind gusts, and a heaping of snow on the Village in the days and hours leading up to the opening ceremonies. The angry climate froze nearby roads and caused debilitating traffic backups that delayed the arrival of officials like then Vice President Richard Nixon. Somehow, though, Mother Nature miraculously changed course, almost simultaneously with the welcoming speech by Olympic Organizing Committee president Prentis Cobb Hale.

At that point, wrote Ancinas, "all eyes looked up to Papoose Peak. The snow had stopped—the sky cleared, fireworks exploded, and thousands of balloons and pigeons [doves of peace] rose up into a blue sky." California then delivered a week of its trademark sunshine to the Games, its participants, and attendees.

There are some who wonder to this day whether Walt Disney and the Walt Disney Company choreographed the weather to perform the magical act it did. While that is debatable, there is no disputing the outsized, unprecedented, and historic imprint Disney made not only on the 1960 Games but on all those that would follow. Disney's influential role in the 1960 Games and the story of the Olympics coming to Squaw Valley is beautifully told in the 2021 documentary *Magic in the Mountains*.

Michael Crawford, a writer and contractor for Disney who helped with archived footage for the documentary and thus was listed as a coproducer, said a combination of factors led to the magical marriage of Disney and the 1960 Olympics. First, he said, "Walt Disney was familiar with the area. He had skied Sugar Bowl and actually invested in the Sugar Bowl Resort and spent quite a bit of time there."

Next came the impeccable timing. The company had just opened Disneyland in 1955, and with ambitions of diversifying into theme parks and beyond, Disney was interested in staging, choreographing, and promoting an Olympic Games. The company "was just getting into outdoor recreation," Crawford said. "They sought to branch out, possibly on the East Coast, and they had an interest in developing a ski resort of their own." Most Olympic Games are money-losers—and sometimes substantially so—and Disney was "willing to take on the financial hit" for doing the Games and providing staff for security and parking. "It was a good experience for them getting into this market."

That "good experience" became an unforgettable one for everyone attending, competing in, and associated with the Games, and much of that is owed to Disney. Crawford recalled that when the horrific weather challenged the opening ceremonies, Disney prophetically decided to forge ahead, saying, "If you live your life like you're supposed to, everything will come out all right."

Disney also brought in Tommy Walker, the head of entertainment, to plan opening-day festivities such as a parade, the release of the birds, and a fireworks display. The decor director, John Hench, designed the iconic Tower of Nations. The principals of Disney were behind "so much of the pageantry," as Crawford put it, which is now repeated at all Summer and Winter Games and likely to be forever linked to the Olympics. All these things were new at the time, brainstormed by the company that has become renowned for its promotional skills and pageantry.

Disney also cashed in on its relationship with Linkletter, with whom it had contracted to put on a "Golden Horseshoe Revue" variety show for athletes and officials jammed into the compact Olympic Village and thirsting for things to do. Other entertainment, celebrity swag, and laughs came courtesy of the biggest stars of the day, including Danny Kaye, Jack Benny, Marlene Dietrich, Red Skelton, Roy Rogers, and Jayne Mansfield. Ancinas called the entertainment and the intimacy "a wonderful accident. There wasn't anything in Squaw Valley, and they had to build an entire Village from scratch. It was a perfect setup."

The cherry on top of the fanfare and the entertainment was an Olympic Games that will be remembered for a flurry of innovations. Courtesy of CBS, it featured a behind-the-scenes use of the instant replay technology that was officially debuted three years later. It was the first time the men's biathlon and women's speed-skating events were staged. It was the first time a downhill racer, Frenchman Jean Vuarnet, won an Alpine event on metal-plastic-wood composite skis.

Oh—and 1960 gave us another fabulous first: the first time a US men's hockey team comprised entirely of amateurs bested powerhouses like Canada, Russia, and Czechoslovakia to claim a gold medal. Yes, a full two decades before 1980, and before Al Michaels's unforgettable tagline, "Do you believe in miracles? Yes!" folks in these parts witnessed what they call the *forgotten* "Miracle on Ice." Its relative anonymity these days "annoys us tremendously," Russell said.

After all that, even the number one doubter of doubters, Brundage, spouted effusive praise of the just-completed Olympic Games. Antonucci's book included Brundage's comments to the Olympic Organizing Committee and the state of California, where he said it took "twenty-five to a hundred years in Europe to accomplish what has been done to a great extent here in four years." Brundage called the 1960 Games "a major success in every respect" and declared he was "pleased—in fact, astonished."

In the decades since 1960, some of the shine has come off those Winter Games, for a few reasons: many facilities built for the Games are gone now; many people who brought the Games to life have lost theirs; and, surprisingly, there is only a small museum to act as a keeper of the rich history connected with the lead-up to, staging of, and record-setting feats during those Games.

For a major museum project, Alex would not have been the go-to

This 1955 photo from Tahoe City epitomizes the amazed and delighted reaction that the community had when Alex Cushing led a successful effort to bring the 1960 Winter Games to Squaw Valley. Credit: Alexandra C. Howard Collection

guy. Both Nancy and Alexandra said Alex made a habit of looking to the future, not behind his shoulder. "He was never one to look back," said Nancy. "He never saved things." Alexandra, who worked at the Metropolitan Museum of Art and shared that she is the "family archivist," agreed that her father didn't look back. "All of that history got lost in a way."

Key players within the Lake Tahoe community and those descendants and historians of the 1960 Games have longed for a place to honor Alex and Wayne, as well as Bill Briner, who was the official photographer for those Games and one of the five men who built the original chairlift at Squaw Valley. Fortunately, there may someday be a place for these men and the memories they made. Antonucci, Ancinas,

Gustafson, Nancy, and many others are on the ground floor of planning and fundraising to build SNOW—the Sierra Nevada Olympic & Winter Sports Museum. The facility will cost between fifteen and twenty million dollars, and the hope is that it will open in the late 2020s.

In what is a fitting way to sum up the beat-the-odds efforts that inspired it, the SNOW Sports Museum website described its mission this way: "We will create a space where local legends can be recognized and celebrated, and where both residents and visitors from all over the world can gather and experience the pioneering spirit that built this magical place."

PART VI

—

HONOR ROLL OF OTHER ATHLETES

CHAPTER 14

A SNAPSHOT OF OTHER OLYMPIC HEROES UNDER THE RADAR

There were a handful of other Olympic athletes I had hoped to profile in this book, given their displays of heroism and the way they embodied the Olympic spirit. While I was not able to connect with them and hear their voices, their stories spoke loudly to me, nonetheless.

- **Abbey D'Agostino Cooper (US) and Nikki Hamblin (New Zealand)—Women's 5,000 Meters, 2016 Summer Olympics, Rio de Janeiro:** In the 2016 Summer Games, America's D'Agostino and New Zealand's Hamblin were trying to earn spots in the women's 5,000-meter finals. With four laps to go in their heat, D'Agostino tripped and collided with Hamblin, who went down. Instead of continuing, D'Agostino helped Hamblin up. But D'Agostino had injured her ankle in the collision, and *she* fell a few steps later. Hamblin then helped D'Agostino up. Hamblin finished twenty-ninth and D'Agostino thirtieth, but that was overshadowed by their dual display of sportsmanship. It was so simple on the one hand—and yet so powerful and uplifting to those who watched. The helping hands and mutual respect the competitors showed each other during a time of struggle is the embodiment of the Olympic spirit.

- **Kieran Behan (Ireland)—Men's Gymnastics, 2016 Summer Olympics, Rio de Janeiro, and 2012 Summer Olympics, London:** Behan was an Irish gymnast who competed in both the 2012 and 2016 Summer Olympics. What he overcame to make it to and compete in the Olympic Games is heroic in my book: a tumor in his leg, stints in a wheelchair, and head and brain injuries that left doctors doubting whether he would walk again, let alone compete at the highest levels.

- **Wojdan Shaherkani (Saudi Arabia)—Women's Judo, 2012 Summer Olympics, London:** Shaherkani and teammate Sarah Attar broke a glass ceiling at the 2012 Summer Games as the first women athletes ever to compete for Saudi Arabia in the Olympic Games. But while Attar had lived in the United States her whole life and competed for Saudi Arabia through dual citizenship, Shaherkani had a more arduous path. She overcame opposition within her own country and stood up to her nation's leaders by insisting (successfully) on her right to wear a hijab during judo competitions.

- **Eric Moussambani (Equatorial Guinea)—Men's Swimming, 2000 Summer Olympics, Sydney:** The first time Moussambani ever saw an Olympic-size swimming pool was, incredibly, at the 2000 Summer Games. He had learned to swim only months before—in a lake and in a hotel swimming pool within his native country, which had a population of fewer than 700,000 at the time of the Games. Moussambani qualified through an IOC "wild-card draw," which was put into place to help encourage Olympic participation by athletes in underdeveloped nations lacking proper training facilities. At those Games, when the only two competitors in his heat of the 100-meter freestyle event were disqualified due to false starts, Moussambani became the lone remaining swimmer in that heat. Despite having just learned how to swim eight months prior and having never swam more than 50 meters, he somehow stayed afloat and finished the race. He became not only a better swimmer but, ultimately, a coach of his country's national swim team.

- **Abdul Baser Wasiqi (Afghanistan)—Men's Marathon, 1996 Summer Olympics, Atlanta:** Wasiqi injured his leg just two weeks prior to the start of the men's marathon at the 1996 Summer Games. Yet he refused to drop out and was nearly an hour and a half behind the second-slowest competitor in the marathon. Still, he completed all 26.2 miles (42 kilometers), limping all the way to the finish line. Wasiqi did not win a medal, but he won great honor for his nation as one of only two competitors from Afghanistan at those Games.

- **Derek Redmond (Great Britain)—Men's 400 Meters, 1992 Summer Olympics, Barcelona:** Redmond had every reason to feel confident about his prospects for the 400 meters at the 1992 Summer Games. He had won an opening heat as well as his quarterfinal race. But 150 meters into the semifinal, a torn hamstring shredded any chance he had of winning. Yet with tremendous determination and a memorable assist from his father, he hobbled to the finish line, completing the race to a thunderous standing ovation. Officially, he had been disqualified—and with this being a semifinal rather than a final, he obviously wasn't going to advance. But all that hardly mattered to those who had seen his brave display of fortitude and his power of perseverance.

ACKNOWLEDGMENTS

The email came a little after 6:00 a.m. on May 10, 2023. *"Hi Doug, I'd be happy to help contribute to your book. You now have my email address. Feel free to contact me when convenient. Cheers."*

It was from Lawrence Lemieux, the former Olympic sailing competitor from Canada and one of over a dozen athletes from multiple countries whom I had hoped to profile for my first book. Lawrence didn't know it at the time, but he had become my icebreaker, and I'll be forever indebted to him for that.

Until then, I had little more than a lofty idea about writing a nonfiction book featuring under-the-radar demonstrations of heroism by Olympic athletes who may not have won medals but who did garner momentary attention and praise before fading out of our collective memories. After weeks of emailing Olympic Committees and national teams and trying to locate athletes via Facebook, Instagram, and LinkedIn, I had very little to show for my efforts.

But after I heard from Lawrence, and David Moorcroft, and the Flaherty family, I began to think I really could convert this idea into reality.

Ultimately, I made enough connections to craft eleven chapters telling the stories of thirteen athletes spread across six continents—men and women who competed in Summer and Winter Olympic Games spanning 1968 to 2022. I also reached key players who were instrumental in the successful bids to bring the 1960 Winter Olympics to Squaw Valley and to restore a Bosnian War–damaged luge and bobsled track from the 1984 Winter Games in Sarajevo. That covered two more chapters.

So, my first and loudest shouts of acknowledgment, thanks, and gratitude go to the athletes, the principals, the family members, and the inner circles of the people I profiled in these thirteen chapters. Without exception, the athletes and other lead actors in this book were incredibly generous with their time and their stories. Not only that, but they were all a pleasure to talk to, despite venturing into this book project without having known me and without any assurances at all, other than hearing a novice book writer tell them he would do his utmost to write about their tales of quiet heroism with conviction, compassion, and candor.

To Manteo Mitchell, Gabriele Andersen-Schiess, David Moorcroft, John Stephen Akhwari, William and Charles Flaherty, Brian Stemmle, Tom Hintnaus, Tracy and Lanny Barnes, Lawrence Lemieux, Mel Wakabayashi, family and friends of Peter Norman, family members and others connected with those involved in the 1960 Squaw Valley Olympics bid, and to Senad and Sabina Omanović and other central players who led the restoration of the 1984 Sarajevo luge and bobsled track, *thank you* is nowhere near enough.

Just as importantly, to the cast of family members, coaches, friends, and inner circles of all those I profiled, you were immeasurably kind and helpful and patient with me. Huge kudos to all of you.

I also profusely thank the team at Girl Friday Productions for helping a naive first-time author turn a raw manuscript into a polished book. Bravo to you for your hard work, eye for detail, editing, fact-checking, double-checking, cover and design work, photo assembly, and more. My beyond-humble thanks to Gail Kretchmer for her editing work and to the GFP team—especially Sara Addicott, Karen Upson, Katie Meyers, Reshma Kooner, Katherine Richards, Roni Greenwood, Mike Hipple, Tiffany Taing, and others who lent me a giant hand.

Also, a mountain of salutes and love to my wife of more than three-and-a-half decades, Teri, who read every one of my chapters without complaint, sat in on production meetings, and nearly always offered an edit or an observation or words of perspective that improved this book.

Additionally, I want to thank my sons, Zach and Cody; my daughter-in-law, Krista; my sister Marcia; my mother-in-law, Connie; extended family members whose support and encouragement meant so much—and a mom, dad, brother, and father-in-law who are no longer on this Earth but are always in my heart.

Finally, my sincere thanks and gratitude to a too-long-to-list group of friends and colleagues whose enthusiasm buoyed me. So many of you encouraged me to pursue this book project, said the topic was worthwhile, and helped give me the motivation and energy to see all this through.

AUTHOR'S NOTES

Following are details regarding sources of information for various chapters of this book, as well as important author's notes regarding the use of interpreters, written Q&A, venue names, etc.

CHAPTER 1—MANTEO MITCHELL

- In recapping the 4×400-meter relay leg that Manteo ran in the semifinals of that 2012 Summer Olympic Games event, I noted his time as 45.7 seconds. Some media reports from the race indicated that Manteo ran a 46.1-second opening leg. However, Manteo verified that the official split time, confirmed by the International Amateur Athletic Federation (IAAF—now known as World Athletics) was 45.7 seconds.

CHAPTER 2—GABRIELE ANDERSEN-SCHIESS

- Gabriele was typically referred to as "Gabriela" in media reports from the 1984 Summer Games, but she goes by and prefers Gabriele.
- Portions of this chapter involve quotes from Jean-François Pahud, the Swiss national coach in charge of middle- and long-distance runners in the 1984 Summer Olympics. Mr. Pahud's quotes are in response to my written questions, which he responded to in French. My sincere thanks to

Gabriele Andersen-Schiess for converting my English questions into French and Pahud's answers back into English.

- Between the original writing of this book and the finished product, I was saddened to learn that Pahud passed away in May 2024, at the age of eighty four.
- References in this chapter to 1984 Olympic women's-marathon winner and former world-record holder Joan Benoit Samuelson use her maiden name, Joan Benoit, as she was known at the time of her gold-medal run. She married her husband, Scott Samuelson, later in 1984.
- *The Geography of Bliss*, to which Erich Steinbock referred, was authored by Eric Weiner and published in January 2008 by Twelve Books. The book contains an entire chapter on the Swiss, including how they are reticent to call attention to themselves or seek out the limelight.

CHAPTER 3—DAVID MOORCROFT

- This chapter contains several quotes from my 2023 interview with John Anderson, the longtime Amateur Athletic Association of England national coach who tutored not only David Moorcroft but numerous other Olympians and world-record holders. Sadly, Anderson died on July 28, 2024. He was ninety-two.

CHAPTER 4—JOHN STEPHEN AKHWARI

- While John speaks some English, his first language is Swahili, and responding to detailed questions was difficult for him. My sincere thanks to Ayoub Laizer, a longtime resident of Tanzania and respected safari guide, who graciously offered to act as the interpreter for my interview with John.
- The *Runner's World* article describing all the physical impacts one faces in running 26.2 miles was published in

the April 12, 2018, issue, written by Jane McGuire and
entitled "14 Things That Happen to Your Body When
You Run a Marathon," https://www.runnersworld
.com/uk/training/marathon/a776113/what-happens-to
-your-body-when-you-run-a-marathon/.

- The *Runner's Blueprint* article that details the effects of a
  severe muscle cramp on distance runners was written by
  David Dack and published September 9, 2023: "Explained:
  The Science Behind Leg Muscle Cramps While Running,"
  https://www.runnersblueprint.com/explained-the-science
  -behind-leg-muscle-cramps-while-running/.
- The overview of what happens when a person dislocates
  a kneecap, and the effect that has, is from the National
  Institutes of Health (NIH), National Library of Medicine,
  updated January 30, 2024: "Overview: Dislocated
  Kneecap," https://www.ncbi.nlm.nih.gov/books
  /NBK561511/.

CHAPTER 10—MEL WAKABAYASHI

- Sadly, Mel died from colon cancer on July 9, 2023, during
  the early writing, researching, and interviewing phases
  of this book. Before he passed away, his son Chris arranged to have Mel answer in writing a series of questions
  I posed to him. Quotes within this chapter attributed to
  Mel are taken from his responses to the Q&A, received
  just before he passed away.
- The historical review of the World War II–era Japanese
  internment camps that I drew upon was from *The
  Canadian Encyclopedia*, published February 15,
  2017: "Internment of Japanese Canadians," https://www
  .thecanadianencyclopedia.ca/en/article/internment
  -of-japanese-canadians.
- The obituary of Mel, from which I quoted, ran in the July
  13, 2023, issue of the *Chatham Daily News*: "Trailblazing
  Chatham Hockey Star Mel Wakabayashi Dies at 80,"

https://www.thecanadianencyclopedia.ca/en/article
/internment-of-japanese-canadians.

CHAPTER 11—PETER NORMAN

- I verified the fact that Australia did not bring any national team male sprinters to the 1972 Olympics in Munich through the following sources: Olympics.com race results and records; the Australia Olympic Committee's historian—via email communication; and *The Peter Norman Story.*
- The fact that Steve Simmons and the USATF team paid for Peter Norman to attend 2000 Olympic Games events, as noted in *The Peter Norman Story*, was verified by Accusplit owner and CEO Ron Sutton via a phone interview. Steve Simmons worked for many years as vice president of Accusplit.
- The retrospective articles on Peter Norman being "shunned" and not being invited to events during the 2000 Summer Games came from an August 3, 2021, profile by Jeff Eisenberg of *Yahoo Sports* and a November 30, 2021, piece by *Sports Illustrated* columnist John Feinstein: "The Forgotten Man: The Story of Peter Norman, the Silver Medalist on the Podium with Tommie Smith and John Carlos," Yahoo Sports; and "On the Monumental, Lasting Impact of Tommie Smith and John Carlos at the 1968 Olympic Games," Literary Hub.
- The fact that Steve Simmons indicated the USATF had never proclaimed a day in honor of an athlete outside the United States was included in media coverage of Peter Norman's funeral, specifically in an October 11, 2006, column by Greg Baum in *The Age.*

CHAPTER 12—SENAD OMANOVIĆ

- Senad speaks limited English, so quotes for this chapter come from a September 18, 2023, Zoom interview conducted with Senad and translated by his daughter, Sabina. Additionally, I relied on written responses to my questions from both Senad and Josef Fendt, the long-time, immediate past president of the International Luge Federation (FIL).

- The descriptions of the lead-up to the Bosnian War and the actions and negotiations to end it came from a recounting of the war written by John Lampe and published in October 2023 for *Encyclopedia Britannica*: "Bosnian War," https://www.britannica.com/event/Bosnian-War.

- The statistic indicating that Sarajevo was the site of as many as 329 shellings a day is from a February 2022 write-up in *Much Better Adventures* magazine that highlighted the initiative to fix up the luge and bobsled track: "A Walk Down the Abandoned Olympic Bobsleigh Track in Sarajevo," https://www.muchbetteradventures.com/magazine/sarajevo-bobsleight-track-winter-olympics/.

- In the paragraph about the luge and bobsled track's challenges in securing resources and gaining attention from BiH, other priorities facing the nation were compiled from a January 5, 2023, article in the *Sarajevo Times*: "What Awaits BiH on the Political Scene in 2023?" https://sarajevotimes.com/what-awaits-bih-on-the-political-scene-in-2023/.

CHAPTER 13—ALEXANDER CUSHING

- In 2020, in recognition of derogatory connotations associated with the term *Squaw*, operators of the former Squaw Valley Resort announced they would be permanently changing its name to Palisades Tahoe. Squaw Valley is used in this chapter for the historical retelling of the story of bringing the 1960 Winter Olympics to the area.

- My thanks to David Antonucci for sharing with me and printing in his book, *Snowball's Chance*, that Lake Tahoe had previously submitted a letter of interest in 1932 in hosting the Winter Olympics, and that there were actually three votes, not two, leading up to the final vote that secured the 1960 Winter Olympics for Squaw Valley.

- My thanks to Nancy Cushing Evans, who shared the information that European nations had predetermined they were going to vote for a location in Austria (Innsbruck) as the site of the 1960 Winter Games.

- My thanks to Alexandra Howard for pointing out that her father, at the time of the effort to bring the 1960 Winter Games to Squaw Valley, was known as Alexander Cushing.

- My thanks to Cindy Gustafson of the Placer County Board of Supervisors, and to her staff, for providing an electronic copy of the board's March 11, 1958, resolution of support for bringing the 1960 Winter Games to Squaw Valley.

- Between the completion of the first manuscript and the published version of this book, I was saddened to learn of the death of Bill Briner. Mr. Briner, who served as the official photographer for the 1960 Winter Games died on June 21, 2024, at age ninety seven. He lived nearly eighty years of his life in the Lake Tahoe area, served twelve years on the Placer County Board of Supervisors, and worked as both the Deputy Director and Director of California State Parks.

ABOUT THE AUTHOR

Doug Levy is a lifelong sports buff and a huge fan of the Olympic Games. He owned and operated a lobbying and government affairs consulting business for twenty-five years, and worked as a sports reporter, sports columnist, and news reporter for the *Tri-City Herald* newspaper in southeast Washington and as a news and politics reporter for *The Columbian* in Vancouver, Washington through much of the 1980s.

He has skydived, run two marathons, climbed a mountain, paraglided, bungee-jumped, and once testified at a murder trial. *Hero Redefined* is his first book.

www.ingramcontent.com/pod-product-compliance
Lightning Source LLC
Chambersburg PA
CBHW020231130626
46549CB00005B/1840